love is a mix tape

T0025800

R.E.M.: "MAN ON THE MOON"

10,000 MANIACS: "CANDY EVERY-
BODY WANTS"

ROYAL TRUX: "SOMETIMES I HANG
MYSELF FROM A TREE"

BETTIE SERVEERT: "PALOMINE"

MORRISSEY: "WE HATE IT WHEN OUR
FRIENDS BECOME SUCCESSFUL"

MARY CHAPIN CARPENTER:
"PASSIONATE KISSES"

love is a mix tape

LIFE
AND LOSS,
ONE
SONG AT
A TIME

**rob
sheffield**

THREE RIVERS PRESS
NEW YORK

Copyright © 2007 by Rob Sheffield

All rights reserved.

Published in the United States by Three Rivers Press, an imprint of the
Crown Publishing Group, a division of Random House, Inc., New York.
www.crownpublishing.com

Three Rivers Press and the Tugboat design are registered trademarks of
Random House, Inc.

Originally published in hardcover in the United States by
Crown Publishers, an imprint of the Crown Publishing Group,
a division of Random House, Inc., New York, in 2007, and
subsequently published in paperback in the United States by
Three Rivers Press, an imprint of the Crown Publishing Group,
a division of Random House, Inc., New York, in 2007.

LIBRARY OF CONGRESS CATALOGING-IN-PUBLICATION DATA

Sheffield, Rob.
  Love is a mix tape/by Rob Sheffield.—1st ed.
  1. Sheffield, Rob. 2. Music critics—United States—Biography.
  3. Journalists—United States—Biography.
  4. Popular music—History and criticism. I. Title.
  ML423.S537A3 2007
  781.64092—dc22
  [B]   2006015248

ISBN 978-1-4000-8303-9

Printed in the United States of America

Design by Barbara M. Bachman

30   29   28   27   26   25   24

for Mom and Dad

I wasted all your precious time
I wasted it all on you.

—PAVEMENT

contents

love is a mix tape

rumblefish

A SIDE ONE DATE/TIME	**B** SIDE TWO DATE/TIME
Pavement: "Shoot the Singer"	• R.E.M.: "Man on the Moon"
The Smiths: "Cemetry Gates"	• 10,000 Maniacs: "Candy Everybody
Belly: "Feed the Tree"	• Wants"
Sloan: "Sugar Tune"	• Royal Trux: "Sometimes"
L7: "Shove"	• Bettie Serveert: "Palomine"
Lois: "Bonds in Seconds"	• Morrissey: "We Hate It When Our
Grenadine: "In a World Without Heroes"	• Friends Become Successful"
The Pooh Sticks: "Sugar Baby"	• Mary Chapin Carpenter: "Passionate
The Chills: "Part Past Part Fiction"	• Kisses"
Whitney Houston: "I'm Every Woman"	• Pavement: "Texas Never Whispers"
L7: "Packin' a Rod"	• Boy George: "The Crying Game"
	• Belly: "Slow Dog"

T*he playback:* late night, Brooklyn, a pot of coffee, and a chair by the window. I'm listening to a mix tape from 1993. Nobody can hear it but me. The neighbors are asleep. The skater kids who sit on my front steps, drink beer, and blast Polish hip-hop—they're gone for the night. The diner next door is closed, but the air is still full of borscht and kielbasa. This is where I live now. A different town, a different apartment, a different year.

This mix tape is just another piece of useless junk that Renée left behind. A category that I guess tonight includes me.

I should have gone to sleep hours ago. Instead, I was rummaging through old boxes, looking for some random paperwork, and I found this tape with her curly scribble on the label. She never played this one for me. She didn't write down the songs, so I have no idea what's in store. But I can already tell it's going to be a late night. It always is. I pop *Rumblefish* into my Panasonic RXC36 boombox on the kitchen counter, pour some more coffee, and let the music have its way with me. It's a date. Just me and Renée and some tunes she picked out.

All these tunes remind me of her now. It's like that old song, "88 Lines About 44 Women." Except it's 8,844 lines about one woman. We've done this before. We get together sometimes, in the dark, share a few songs. It's the closest we'll get to hearing each other's voices tonight.

The first song: Pavement's "Shoot the Singer." Just a sad California boy, plucking his guitar and singing about a girl he likes. They were Renée's favorite band. She used to say, "There's a lot of room in my dress for these boys."

Renée called this tape *Rumblefish*. I don't know why. She recorded it over a promo cassette by some band called Drunken Boat, who obviously didn't make a big impression, because she stuck her own label over their name, put Scotch tape over the punch holes, and made her own mix. She dated it "Ides o' March 1993." She also wrote this inspirational credo on the label:

"You know what I'm doing—just follow along!"

—JENNIE GARTH

Ah, the old Jennie Garth workout video, *Body in Progress.* Some nights you go to the mall with your squeeze, you're both a little wasted, and you come home with a Jennie Garth workout video. That's probably buried in one of these boxes, too. Neither of us ever threw anything away. We made a lot of mix tapes while we were together. Tapes for making out, tapes for dancing, tapes for falling asleep. Tapes for doing the dishes, for walking the dog. I kept them all. I have them piled up on my bookshelves, spilling out of my kitchen cabinets, scattered all over the bedroom floor. I don't even have pots or pans in my kitchen, just that old boombox on the counter, next to the sink. So many tapes.

I met Renée in Charlottesville, Virginia, when we were both twenty-three. When the bartender at the Eastern Standard put on a tape, Big Star's *Radio City*, she was the only other person in the room who perked up. So we drank bourbon and talked about music. We traded stories about the bands we liked, shows we'd seen. Renée loved the Replacements and Alex Chilton and the Meat Puppets. So did I.

I loved the Smiths. Renée hated the Smiths.

The second song on the tape is "Cemetry Gates" by The Smiths.

The first night we met, I told her the same thing I've told every single girl I've ever had a crush on: "I'll make you a tape!" Except this time, with this girl, it worked. When we were planning our wedding a year later, she said that instead of stepping on a glass at the end of the ceremony, she wanted to step on a cassette case, since that's what she'd been doing ever since she met me.

Falling in love with Renée was not the kind of thing you walk away from in one piece. I had no chance. She put a hitch in my git-along. She would wake up in the middle of the night and say things like "What if Bad Bad Leroy Brown was a girl?" or "Why don't they have commercials for salt like they do for milk?" Then she would fall back to sleep, while I would lie awake and give thanks for this alien creature beside whom I rested.

Renée was a real cool hell-raising Appalachian punk-rock girl. Her favorite song was the Rolling Stones' "Let's Spend the Night Together." Her favorite album was Pavement's *Slanted and Enchanted*. She rooted for the Atlanta Braves and sewed her own silver vinyl pants. She knew which kind of screwdriver was which. She baked pies, but not very often. She could rap Roxanne Shante's "Go on Girl" all the way through. She called Eudora Welty "Miss Eudora." She had an MFA in fiction and never got any stories published, but she kept writing them anyway. She bought too many shoes and dyed her hair red. Her voice was full of the frazzle and crackle of music.

Renée was a country girl, three months older than me. She was born on November 21, 1965, the same day as Björk, in the

Metropolitan Mobile Home Park in Northcross, Georgia. She grew up in southwest Virginia, with her parents, Buddy and Nadine, and her little sister. When she was three, Buddy was transferred to the defense plant in Pulaski County, and so her folks spent a summer building a house there. Renée used to sit in the backyard, feeding grass to the horses next door through the fence. She had glasses, curly brown hair, and a beagle named Snoopy. She went to Fairlawn Baptist Church and Pulaski High School and Hollins College. She got full-immersion baptized in Claytor Lake. The first record she ever owned was KC & the Sunshine Band's "Get Down Tonight." KC was her first love. I was her last.

I was a shy, skinny, Irish Catholic geek from Boston. I'd never met anybody like Renée before. I moved to Charlottesville for grad school, my plans all set: go down South, get my degree, then haul ass to the next town. The South was a scary new world. The first time I saw a possum in my driveway, I shook a bony fist at the sky and cursed this godforsaken rustic hellhole. I'm twenty-three! Life is passing me by! My ancestors spent centuries in the hills of County Kerry, waist-deep in sheep shit, getting shot at by English soldiers, and my grandparents crossed the ocean in coffin ships to come to America, just so I could get possum rabies?

Renée had never set foot north of Washington, D.C. For her, Charlottesville was the big bad city. She couldn't believe her eyes, just because there were *sidewalks* everywhere. Her ancestors were Appalachians from the hills of West Virginia; both of her grandfathers were coal miners. We had nothing in common, except we both loved music. It was the first connection we had, and we depended on it to keep us together. We did a lot of work to meet in the middle. Music brought us together. So now music was stuck with us.

I was lucky I got to be her guy for a while.

I remember this song. L7, punk-rock girls from L.A., the "Shove" single on Sub Pop. Renée did a Spin *cover story on them, right after she made this tape. She'd never seen California before. The girls in the band took her shopping and picked out some jeans for her.*

When we were married we lived in Charlottesville, in a moldy basement dump that flooded every time it rained. We often drove her creaky 1978 Chrysler LeBaron through the mountains, kicking around junk shops, looking for vinyl records and finding buried treasures on scratched-up 45s for a quarter a pop. She drove me up to the Meadow Muffin on Route 11, outside Stuart's Draft, for the finest banana milkshakes on the planet. Every afternoon, I picked Renée up from work. By night we'd head to Tokyo Rose, the local sushi bar, where bands played in the basement. We went to hear every band that came to town, whether we liked them or not. If we'd waited around for famous, successful, important bands to play Charlottesville, we would have been waiting a long time. Charlottesville was a small town; we had to make our own fun. Renée would primp for the shows, sew herself a new skirt. We knew we would see all of our friends there, including all the rock boys Renée had crushes on. The bassist—always the bassist. I'm six-five, so I would hang in the back with the other tall rock dudes and lean against the wall. Renée was five-two, and she definitely wasn't the type of gal to hang in the back, so she'd dart up front and run around and wag her tail. She made a scene. She would dive right into the crowd and let me just linger behind her, basking in her glow. Any band that was in town, Renée would invite them to crash at our place, even though there wasn't even enough room for us.

Belly? Aaaargh! Renée! Why are you doing this to me? This band blows homeless goats. I can't believe she liked this song enough to tape it.

I get sentimental over the music of the '90s. Deplorable, really. But I love it all. As far as I'm concerned, the '90s was the best era for music ever, even the stuff that I loathed at the time, even the stuff that gave me stomach cramps. Every note from those years is charged with life for me now. For instance, I hated Pearl Jam at the time. I thought they were pompous blowhards. Now, whenever a Pearl Jam song comes on the car radio, I find myself pounding my fist on the dashboard, screaming, "Pearl JAM! Pearl JAM! Now *this* is rock and roll! Jeremy's SPO-ken! But he's still al-LIIIIIIVE!"

I don't recall making the decision to love Pearl Jam. Hating them was a lot more fun.

1991. The year punk broke. The palindrome year. In the *Planet of the Apes* movies, it was the year of the ape revolution, but I'll settle for the 1991 we got. This was the year we got married. We knew it would be a big deal, and it was. The next few years were a rush. It was a glorious time for pop culture, the decade of Nirvana and Lollapalooza and *Clueless* and *My So-Called Life* and

Sassy and *Pulp Fiction* and Greg Maddux and Garth Brooks and
Green Day and Drew and Dre and Snoop and *Wayne's World*. It
was the decade Johnny Depp got his *Winona Forever* tattoo, the
decade Beavis and Butthead got butt-shaped tattoos on their
butts. It was the decade of Kurt Cobain and Shania Twain and
Taylor Dayne and Brandy Chastain. The boundaries of American culture were exploding, and music was leading the way.

There was a song Renée and I made up in the car, singing
along with the radio.

> *Out on the road today, I saw a Sub Pop sticker on a Subaru.*
> *A little voice inside my head said, yuppies smell teen spirit too.*
> *I thought I knew what love was, but I was blind.*
> *Those days are gone forever, whatever, never mind.*

At the end of the working day, we rubbed each other's feet and
sang Pavement songs to each other, and we knew every word
was true, even the one that went, "Fruit covered nails/Electricity
and lust." I rubbed Lubriderm into her pantyhose burns. The
Reagan-Bush nightmare was coming to an end, so close we
could taste it. Nirvana was all over the radio. Corporate rock was
dead. On *90210*, Dylan and Kelly were making out on the beach
to "Damn, I Wish I Was Your Lover." We were young and in love
and the world was changing.

When we weren't being students or working lame jobs, we
were rock critics, freelancing for the *Village Voice* and *Spin* and

Option. Our friends in other towns had fanzines, so we wrote for them, too. We were DJs on our local independent radio station, WTJU. Bands that would have been too weird, too feminist, too rough for the mainstream a year earlier suddenly *were* the mainstream, making their noise in public. Our subcultural secrets were out there, in the world, where they belonged. After work, Renée and I would cruise by Plan 9 Records and flip through the vinyl 45s. There was always something new we *had* to hear. We wrote as fast as we could, but still there was more great music out there than we had time to write about. Sometimes we got checks in the mail for writing, so we bought more records. Renée would hunker down over her typewriter and play the same Bratmobile single for hours, flipping it over every two and a half minutes, singing along: "If you be my bride, we can kiss and ride / We can have real fun, we can fuck and run." Everything was changing, that was obvious. The world was so full of music, it seemed we could never run out. 'Twas bliss in that dawn to be alive, but to be young and overworked and underexposed and stuck in a nowhere town was very heaven. It was our time, the first one we had to ourselves.

It was a smashing time, and then it ended, because that's what times do.

Whitney Houston, "I'm Every Woman." Mmmmm. Whitney was so rad back then. What the hell happened?

Renée left a big mess behind: tapes, records, shoes, sewing patterns, piles of fabric she was planning to turn into skirts and handbags. Fashion mags and rock fanzines she was in the middle of reading. Novels jammed with bookmarks. Drafts of stories all over her desk. Pictures she'd ripped from magazines and taped up on the walls—Nirvana, PJ Harvey, John Travolta, Drew Barrymore, Shalom Harlow, Mo Vaughn. A framed photo of the 1975 Red Sox. A big clay Mexican sun god she brought back from doing the L7 story in L.A. A stuffed pumpkin head from—well, no idea. Nutty things she sewed for herself, mod minidresses from fabric she found with little snow peas or Marilyn Monroe faces all over. She was in the middle of everything, living her big, messy, epic life, and none of us who loved her will ever catch up with her.

Renée loved to *do* things. That was mysterious to me, since I was more comfortable talking about things and never doing them. She liked passion. She liked adventure. I cowered from passion and talked myself out of adventure. Before I met her, I was just another hermit wolfboy, scared of life, hiding in my room with my records and my fanzines. One of Renée's friends asked her, "Does your boyfriend wear glasses?" She said, "No, he wears a Walkman." I was a wallflower who planned to stay that way, who never imagined anybody else to be. Suddenly, I got all tangled up in this girl's noisy, juicy, sparkly life. Without her, I didn't want to do anything, except keep being good at Renée. You know the story about Colonel Tom Parker, after Elvis died? The Colonel said, "Hell, I'll keep right on managing him." That's how I felt. Every tree in the woods, every car that passed me on the road, every song on the radio, all seemed to be Gloria Grahame at the end of *The Big Heat*, asking the same question: "What was your wife like?" It was the only conversation I was interested in.

Our friend Suzle told me her sister didn't understand—she always thought Suzle had one friend named "Robin Renée." How did Robin Renée turn into Rob and Renée, two different people?

The whole world got cheated out of Renée. I got cheated less than anybody, since I got more of her than anybody. But still, I wanted more of her. I wanted to be her guy forever and ever. I always pictured us growing old together, like William Holden and Ernest Borgnine in *The Wild Bunch*, side by side in our sleeping bags, drinking coffee and planning the next payroll heist. We only got five years. On our fifth anniversary, we drove out to Afton Mountain and checked into a motel. We got righteously wasted and blasted David Bowie's "Five Years" over and over. It's a song about how the world is going to end in five years, which forces everybody to seize the freedom to do whatever they want, to act out their craziest desires and devour the moment and not even think about the future.

"Five years!" we screamed in unison. "That's *aaaooowwwlll* we got!"

It *was* all we got. That was a good night. There were a lot of good nights. We got more of those than we had any right to expect, five years' worth, but I wanted more, anyway.

Another L7 song, "Packin' a Rod." It's a cover of an old L.A. hardcore punk anthem—Renée could have told you who did the original version, but I can't. And already we're at the end of side one. Eject. Flip it.

It's too late to sleep anyway. The coffee's gone cold, so I just heat up another pot. Tonight, I feel like my whole body is made out of memories. I'm a mix tape, a cassette that's been rewound so many times you can hear the fingerprints smudged on the tape.

Press play.

First song, side two: R.E.M.'s "Man on the Moon." Did Renée ever make a mix tape without R.E.M.? A whole generation of southern girls, raised on the promise of Michael Stipe.

I now get scared of forgetting anything about Renée, even the tiniest detail, even the bands on this tape I can't stand—if she touched them, I want to hear her fingerprints. Sometimes, I wake up in the middle of the night, my heart pounding, trying to remember: What was Renée's shoe size? What color were her eyes? What was her birthday, her grandparents' first names, that Willie Nelson song we heard on the radio in Atlanta? The memory comes back, hours or days later. It always comes back. But in the moment, I panic. I'm positive it's gone for good. I'm shaking from that sensation now, trying to remember some of this music. Nothing connects to the moment like music. I count on the music to bring me back—or, more precisely, to bring her forward.

There are some songs on this tape that nobody else on the planet remembers. I guarantee it. Like the Grenadine song "In a

World Without Heroes." Grenadine wasn't even a real band—just a goofball side project. As far as we were concerned, though, this was easily the finest pseudo-Bowie limp-wristed fuzz-guitar indie-boy girl-worship ballad of 1992. We never convinced anyone else to agree. Not even our so-called friends would lie to us about this one.

Nobody ever liked it except me and Renée, and now she's gone, which means nobody remembers it. Not even the guy who wrote it. I know that for a fact, because Mark Robinson played a solo show at Tokyo Rose a few years later. When he asked for requests, we screamed for "In a World Without Heroes." He just stared and shook his head. A few songs later, with a little more liquid courage in us, we screamed for it again. He stopped asking for requests. So it's official: *nobody* likes this song.

A song nobody likes is a sad thing. But a love song nobody likes is hardly a thing at all.

Mary Chapin Carpenter. A big country-radio hit at the time. Wasn't she the one who wore leg-warmers?

The country singers understand. It's always that one song that gets you. You can hide, but the song comes to find you. Country singers are always twanging about that number on the jukebox they can't stand to hear you play, the one with the memories. If you're George Jones, it's 4-0-3-3. If you're Olivia Newton-John, it's B-17. If you're Johnny Paycheck, you can't stop yourself from going back to the bar where they play that song over and over, where they have a whole jukebox full of those songs. Johnny Paycheck called it "The Meanest Jukebox in Town."

Gangsters understand, too. In the old gangster movies, you're always running away to a new town, somewhere they won't know your mug shot. You can bury the dirty deeds of your past. Except the song follows you. In *Detour*, it's "I Can't Believe You're in Love with Me." The killer hears it on the truck-stop jukebox, and he realizes there's no escape from the girl. In *Gilda*, it's "Put the Blame on Mame." In *Dark Passage*, it's "Too Marvelous for Words." Barbara Stanwyck in *Clash by Night,* she's so cool and tough and unflappable, until she goes to a bar and gets jumped by a song on the jukebox, "I Hear a Rhapsody." She starts to ramble about a husband who died, and a small town where she used to sell sheet music. She's not so tough now. You can't get away from the meanest jukebox in town.

Pavement again. "Texas Never Whispers." One of our favorites. The tape creaks a little. I know it must be getting near the end.

I've been playing *Rumblefish* all night. By now, I know all the tunes. I'm writing down their titles, so I won't forget. I'm still staring out the window, but the sun won't rise for another couple of hours. The city lights are blinking through the trees of McCarren Park. The house across the street has a stuffed wooden owl whose head spins around every fifteen minutes, which is extremely annoying. The city is full of adventure, just a couple of subway stops away. But I'm not going anywhere.

We met on September 17, 1989. We got married on July 13, 1991. We were married for five years and ten months. Renée died on May 11, 1997, very suddenly and unexpectedly, at home with me, of a pulmonary embolism. She was thirty-one. She's buried in Pulaski County, Virginia, on the side of a hill, next to the Wal-Mart.

As soon as Side Two cuts off, right in the middle of a terrible Belly song, I sit there and wait for the final *ca-chunka*. Then I flip the tape and press play again. The first song is Pavement's "Shoot the Singer," which I just heard an hour ago. I have some unfinished business with these tunes. I'm going to be up for a while. Renée's not done with me yet.

hey jude

APRIL 1979

A SIDE ONE DATE/TIME	**B** SIDE TWO DATE/TIME
The Beatles: "Hey Jude"	The Beatles: "Hey Jude"

One night when I was twelve, my dad and I went out to Howard Johnson's for hot chocolate. The jukebox in the booth offered two songs for a quarter, so we each picked one. I punched up my latest fave, Toto's "Hold the Line." My dad picked something I'd never heard before called "Duke of Earl," and he got real excited as that "duke, duke, duke" started bleating out of the speakers. I rolled my eyes as he sang along, but I thought to myself, Well this *is* kind of better than "Hold the Line."

As my Dad and I sat around the house one Saturday afternoon, playing Beatles records, we started batting around the idea that it was theoretically possible to loop a version of "Hey Jude" long enough to fill up an entire cassette. All we had to do was press pause and lift the needle every once in a while, and fiddle with the volume knobs. A few hours later, we had a ninety-minute tape of "na na nas," along with many "yeah yeah yeahs" and a few "Judy Judy Judy wows." We listened to the playback, and I could not believe what we had accomplished. This was a new Beatles song that hadn't existed before. It was Something New, as the Beatles would say. The difference between Yesterday . . . and Today. My dad and I had built model airplanes together, gone to Red Sox games. But listening to this tape, I knew it was our greatest hit. Paul McCartney couldn't have been more proud after writing the actual song.

I listen to *Hey Jude* now, and I think two things: I never want to hear this song again, and in 1979, my dad was around the age I am now, and given a Saturday afternoon he could have spent any way he pleased, he chose to spend it with his twelve-year-old son, making this ridiculous little tape. He probably forgot about it the next day. But I didn't.

There are all kinds of mix tapes. There is always a reason to make one.

The Party Tape

Par-tay! You know what that means—hours to create the perfect party tape, plus ten minutes to clean the house and pour all the two-thirds-empty liquor bottles into a bowl of Crystal Light and call it Orange Lotus Surprise Blossom. Then, after the party's over, you hold on to the tape. You never know when you might get a call, saying, "Dude, party tonight! Bring a tape!" You always make sure to keep a dance tape or two handy in your room, JUST IN CASE, because YOU NEVER KNOW, the same way Cosmo girls keep a spare bottle of bubbly in the fridge. A few friends are over having drinks, a song comes on, a couple girls start to dance, and you don't want it to fizzle out, do you? One summer in Charlottesville, I had these upstairs neighbors, Wally and Drew, whose mix tapes were neurobiologically engineered to get their girlfriends to make out with each other. I saw it happen. The tape goes in, Jeff Buckley moans one of his ten-minute thingies, then his falsetto fades into the guitar intro of Marvin Gaye's "Let's Get It On," and bam—their girlfriends are lap-dancing each other like brazen little colts. Those guys knew how to make a party tape.

I Want You

Always a great reason to make a tape.

We're Doing It? Awesome!

An even better reason to make a tape. This is when you start trading tapes of songs like Shalamar's "Dancing in the Sheets" or the Staple Singers' "Let's Do It Again" or My Bloody Valentine's "Soft as Snow (But Warm Inside)." Sad, really. I have reason to believe I was once dumped for giving a girl a tape with one of my favorite mushy '80s R&B ballads, Gregory Abbott's "Shake You Down." Never tried that again. These tapes are one of the primary perks of being in a relationship, along with the free haircuts. Some couples stop making each other tapes—I have no idea what happens to them.

You Like Music, I Like Music, I Can Tell We're Going to Be Friends

You just met somebody. You're talking about the songs you like. Oh, yeah, that band! Ever hear this band? You would *love* this song. I'll make you a tape! Frequently confused with the "I Want You" tape by the giving or receiving party, resulting in hijinks and hilarity all around.

You Broke My Heart and Made Me Cry
and Here Are Twenty or Thirty Songs
About It

The best ever was the "Is She Really Going Out With Him?" mix, which my friend Heather's boyfriend Charles made while they were going through what is spinelessly referred to as a "transitional period." It began with the Violent Femmes' "Please Please Please Do Not Go," and then it got desperate— lovelorn boys begging for more punishment: Elvis Costello's "Why Don't You Love Me (Like You Used To Do)?", The English Beat's "Hands Off She's Mine," Don Henley's "Boys of Summer." It worked, though—it got them back together. Heather kept playing it for all her friends, right in front of Charles; she was proud she could put him through that kind of misery, and I guess he was proud, too. Twenty years later, they're living in Utah, married, with four kids who owe their *lives* to this tape. Scary.

The Road Trip

My friend Jane came to visit me in Boston the year after college, when she was living in Southern California. She wanted me to drive her around town all night, so she made a tape for the occasion. Every song got permanently fried into my brain. We hit the Southeast Expressway to Van Morrison's "Friday's Child." We cruised Castle Island to Peter Green's "Man of the World." We sang along to the Rolling Stones' "Ventilator Blues," Muddy Waters's "Stuff You Gotta Watch," the Jam's "Life Through a Window," and so many others. We drove all night, spinning that tape through Dorchester and Southie and Watertown and JP. When the sun was coming up, we tossed the tape out the window. I haven't seen Jane in years, but now I hang out at a bar in Brooklyn called Daddy's, where they have "Friday's Child" on the jukebox. Every time I'm there playing the Elvis pinball machine, I hit "Friday's Child," number 9317, and send it out to a faraway friend, wherever she is.

No Hard Feelings, Babe

Renée always swore her best friend in high school would break up with girls by taping "Free Bird" for them. A guy I knew in college dumped his ladies by taping Bob Dylan's "Don't Think Twice, It's All Right" for them. In college I once thought I was breaking up with a girl by giving her a tape that began with Roxy Music's "The Thrill of It All." It took a few days for me to realize that she had no idea we were broken up, which I guess means it didn't work. Why do people do this? Asshologists, please advise.

I Hate This Fucking Job

You know how sometimes you're reading the paper with a boysenberry muffin and an iced soy cran-mocha colada and you notice the kids behind the counter screaming along with Fear's "Fresh Flesh" or Drunks with Guns' "Blood Bath"? Just their special way of reminding you that *they hate this fucking job*.

The Radio Tape

Back when people listened to the radio, you kept a tape handy in your boombox at all times so you could capture the hot new hits of the week. The intro would always get cut off, and the DJ would chatter over the end. You also ended up with static, commercials, and jingles, but all that noise just added to the field-recording verisimilitude. The radio tape puts you right back in the original time and place when you first heard the songs. You are *there*, my friend. A girl I knew once had a radio tape with "Rock Me Amadeus" five or six times on each side; she just pressed record every time she heard it.

The Walking Tape

Some people like to make workout tapes and take them to the gym, but I can't fathom why. Any music I hear in a gym is ruined forever. I do like to take a lot of walks, though, which require long, mumble-trance guitar songs. Any time I hear the Byrds or Buffalo Springfield, I remember one spring day in Charlottesville when I accidentally climbed Dudley Mountain on the outskirts of town—I didn't know it was a mountain until I was on top of it, and the only way off was to walk back down. I had only one tape in my Walkman, so I listened to it continuously, end to end, for about ten hours. The opening strum of the Byrds' "What's Happening" still makes my legs ache.

There are lots more where these came from. The drug tape. The commute tape. The dishes tape. The shower tape. The collection of good songs from bad albums you don't ever want to play again. The greatest hits of your significant other's record pile, the night before you break up. There are millions of songs in the world, and millions of ways to connect them into mixes. Making the connections is part of the fun of being a fan.

I believe that when you're making a mix, you're making history. You ransack the vaults, you haul off all the junk you can carry, and you rewire all your ill-gotten loot into something new. You go through an artist's entire career, zero in on that one moment that makes you want to jump and dance and smoke bats and bite the heads off drugs. And then you play that one moment over and over.

A mix tape steals these moments from all over the musical cosmos, and splices them into a whole new groove.

Walter Benjamin, in his prescient 1923 essay "One Way Street," said a book was an outdated means of communication between two boxes of index cards. One professor goes through books, looking for tasty bits he can copy onto index cards. Then he types his index cards up into a book, so other professors can go through it and copy tasty bits onto their own index cards.

Benjamin's joke was: Why not just sell the index cards? I guess
that's why we trade mix tapes. We music fans love our classic
albums, our seamless masterpieces, our *Blonde on Blondes* and
our *Talking Books*. But we love to pluck songs off those albums
and mix them up with other songs, plunging them back into the
rest of the manic slipstream of rock and roll. I'd rather hear the
Beatles' "Getting Better" on a mix tape than on *Sgt. Pepper* any
day. I'd rather hear a Frank Sinatra song between Run-DMC
and Bananarama than between two other Frank Sinatra songs.
When you stick a song on a tape, you set it free.

Most mix tapes are CDs now, yet people still call them mix
tapes. The technology changes, but the spirit is the same. I can
load up my iPod with weeks' worth of music and set it on shuf-
fle to play a different mix every time. I can borrow somebody
else's iPod and pack it with songs I think they'd like. I can talk
to a friend on the phone, mention a couple of songs, down-
load them on LimeWire while we're talking, and listen together.
The hip-hop world now thrives on mix tapes, with artists circu-
lating their rhymes on the street via bootleg CDs. They're never
technically tapes, but they're always called mix tapes anyway,
just because tapes are always cool.

It's a fundamental human need to pass music around, and
however the technology evolves, the music keeps moving.
Renée's dad, Buddy, has a file on his hard drive that his cousin
Jerry e-mailed to him. It's reel-to-reel tapes from his parents'
house back in West Virginia, from the 1950s, with Papaw playing guitar and the kids harmonizing. Back then they would sit

around and sing all night. Buddy and his brothers sang The
Sons of the Pioneers' "Cool Water." Mamaw would always sing
her favorite, Hank Snow's "Wedding Bells." Papaw would serenade Mamaw with some of the old Merle Travis songs, like "Fat
Gal" and "I Like My Chicken Fryin' Size." Renée told me about
these nights when she was a little girl, the long summer nights
when she would lie on the floor in her grandparents' house and
listen to her aunt and uncles sing these ancient songs. She never
got to hear any of these home recordings, though, because by
the 1970s nobody had reel-to-reel players anymore, so they
were sitting around unheard. After she died, Cousin Jerry found
the old tapes, digitized them, and e-mailed them around. Buddy
can now sit at his computer and go back to a shack in West Virginia, listening to his father sing "So Round, So Firm, So Fully
Packed" to his mother.

I listen to music practically every waking hour. I'm a writer
for *Rolling Stone*, which means my typical workday is going to
hear bands play and listening to records. I have lived the absurd
life of a rock journalist. I have seen Aerosmith call room service
to order incense, and I've seen them deal with a ringing hotel-
room phone by ripping it out of the wall. I have listened to Brit-
ney Spears freak out in the back of a limo on her cell phone. I
was in an elevator with Madonna once. I have eaten french fries
on the tour bus with Linkin Park, shared hangover cures with
Ryan Adams, debated Dylan lyrics with Richard Gere, sung
karaoke with the Yeah Yeah Yeahs. I have smoked pot at the
SoHo Grand Hotel with Massive Attack (I won't be doing that

again—damn, those guys had some strong pot). On MTV, Carson Daly introduced me as "the man who knows music the way the Naked Chef knows beef stroganoff," and although I remain unsure of what he meant by that, I feel strongly that it was a compliment. I've watched myself on VH1, talking about filthy Frankie Goes to Hollywood lyrics, in front of my mom—that sucked. Billy Corgan and Scott Weiland have denounced me. Garbage's Shirley Manson criticized my haircut. She was right, too—that haircut was crap. Did I mention I was in an elevator with Madonna once?

I have built my entire life around loving music, and I surround myself with it. I'm always racing to catch up on my next favorite song. But I never stop playing my mixes. Every fan makes them. The times you lived through, the people you shared those times with—nothing brings it all to life like an old mix tape. It does a better job of storing up memories than actual brain tissue can do. Every mix tape tells a story. Put them together, and they add up to the story of a life.

roller boogie

DECEMBER 1979

A SIDE ONE DATE/TIME	**B** SIDE TWO DATE/TIME
Van Halen: "Dance the Night Away"	• M: "Pop Muzik"
Gary Numan: "Cars"	• Michael Jackson: "Don't Stop Till You
J. Geils Band: "I Could Hurt You"	• Get Enough"
Donna Summer: "Dim All the Lights"	• J. Geils Band: "Musta Got Lost"
Cheap Trick: "Surrender"	• The Knack: "My Sharona"
ELO: "Turn to Stone"	• Pink Floyd: "Another Brick in the Wall"
Blondie: "Heart of Glass"	• Rolling Stones: "Wild Horses"
Boston: "Don't Look Back"	• Michael Jackson: "Off the Wall"
Donna Summer: "Bad Girls"	• Aerosmith: "Dream On"
Foreigner: "Feels Like the First Time"	• Earth Wind & Fire: "September"
Lynyrd Skynyrd: "Free Bird"	• J. Geils Band: "Give It to Me"
	• Led Zeppelin: "Stairway to Heaven"

L*ike a lot of stories,* this one begins, "I was too young to know better." Like a lot of stories that begin "I was too young to know better," this one involves Cheap Trick.

I'm a man of few regrets. Of course I regret paying money to see *Soul Plane,* and I regret taking a bus trip through scenic Pennsylvania Dutch country once, when I could have stayed home and watched MTV's David Lee Roth Weekend. (There'll be plenty of other David Lee Roth Weekends, I told myself. What was I thinking?) But most of all, I regret turning thirteen, and staying that way for the next ten years or so. Every time I dig up one of the tapes from my adolescence, it's like making the Stations of the Cross, reliving one excruciatingly bad move after another.

Roller Boogie is a relic from—when else?—the '70s. This is a tape I made for the eighth-grade dance. The tape still plays, even if the cogs are a little creaky and the sound quality is dismal. It's a ninety-minute TDK Compact Cassette, and like everything else made in the '70s, it's beige. It takes me back to the fall of 1979, when I was a shy, spastic, corduroy-clad Catholic kid from the suburbs of Boston, grief-stricken over the '78 Red Sox. The words "douche" and "bag" have never coupled as passionately as they did in the person of my thirteen-year-old self. My body, my brain, my elbows that stuck out like switchblades, my feet that got tangled in my bike spokes, but most of all my soul— these formed the waterbed where douchitude and bagness made love sweet love with all the feral intensity of Burt Reynolds and Rachel Ward in *Sharky's Machine*.

The only reason I ran for student council was so I'd get to be on the social activities committee, which meant planning the only part of the social activities I really cared about: the music. We got three dances that year, and I got the plum job of making the dance tapes.

It went without saying that I had to include "Free Bird" and "Stairway to Heaven." The other selections were mine. As you can see from the playlist above, I knew school dances about as well as I knew tantric sex. *Roller Boogie* holds some of the least danceable grooves ever passed off in the name of getting down. Jesus H. Christ on ice and Mary in the penalty box! Why did I put Boston's "Don't Look Back" on a dance tape? Why did I think anybody would shake ass to ELO? Why was I not tarred and feathered by my classmates by the time the *third* J. Geils Band song came on?

But hey, I was the only kid who wanted the job, and I took it seriously. I borrowed records from people at school, kids who ordinarily would have sooner trusted me with their tooth-brushes, retainers, and headgear than with their records. I immersed myself in the glorious masterpieces of the seventies, such as side one of the first Boston album, Led Zeppelin, Van Halen, and side two of the first Boston album. I came to regard the J. Geils Band's second live album as vastly inferior to the first. I wondered what the lyrics of "Stairway to Heaven" meant.

I had never made out, smoked, drank, broken a law, set fire to a car, vandalized a cemetery, or worn socks that matched. But I had the passion for rock and roll; I was a regular Dr. Johnny Fever in the body of a Les Nessman. Nobody could truly under-stand my quest to rock—except maybe Annie, my favorite *Solid Gold* dancer. I was totally clueless about social interaction, and completely scared of girls. All I knew was that music was going to make girls fall in love with me.

So I approached my beatmaster duties with the same rever-ence I brought to my Sundays as an altar boy serving Mass. I approached my stereo sanctuary and genuflected. I lifted each vinyl wafer to the heavens. I unveiled the cassette ostentorium: "Take this, all of you, and rock. This is the blood of the new and everlasting covenant. It will be shed for you, and for all who rock, so that rock may be worshiped and glorified."

Heidi From Algebra pulled me aside in the hallway and handed me her copy of the Rolling Stones' *Hot Rocks*. She didn't even crack a smile. "'Wild Horses,'" she told me. "It's a slow dance. The girls like it." She wouldn't let go of the record until I gave her a "Wild Horses" guarantee, and then she disappeared down the hall. It was the only conversation we ever had.

"Rock, I am not worthy to receive you. But only say the word, and I shall be healed."

"Nobody cares about the music at these things, you know," my dad told me. "They go to meet girls." I chuckled. Oh, Dad, you are so out of it.

The dilemma of the eighth-grade dance is that boys and girls use music in different ways. Girls enjoy music they can dance to, music with strong vocals and catchy melodies. Boys, on the other hand, enjoy music they can improve by making up filthy new lyrics, as in: "Girl, you really got me goin', I don't know who you're blowin'," or "Eleanor Rigby, blowing the groom in a church where a wedding has been," or "Something in the way she blows me," or "And though she was born a long, long time ago, your mother should blow." And blow on.

I listened to rock station WCOZ in eighth grade, and slept under a WCOZ poster that depicted a giant space robot who used a light saber to slash "94.5 FM" into the very fabric of the galaxy. I had rock-and-roll parents, who played the Famous Jim Sands Oldies show on WBZ all the time. They used to slow-dance in the kitchen to songs like "In the Still of the Nite." They watched *Happy Days* with us and explained that the Fonz was not really so cool because he liked Frankie Avalon. In our house, the radio was always on. Even our babysitter Regina, a crazy old Irish lady from Dorchester, used to chain-smoke in the kitchen and sing along with Dionne Warwick at the top of her tarry lungs, when she wasn't offering my sisters dating advice such as "Never give 'em anything for free."

I had three little sisters—Ann, Tracey, and Caroline—and we were all devoted to our radios. We bought our first record together, chipping in two bucks apiece and ordering *The Best of the Monkees* off of TV. I adored the Monkees, but I was terrified of Mickey Dolenz. For some reason, I got the notion in my head that Mickey Dolenz was what happened if you smoked pot—you made screwy faces, you talked too loud, you bugged every-body. I was convinced Mickey got this way from drugs, which also explained his dashiki—he was obviously a nice Irish boy gone wrong. I suspect that over the course of my life, my chemi-cal experimentation has been severely curtailed by the specter of Mickey Dolenz.

Ann and Tracey were on the basketball team, so they learned cool dances to go with disco tunes like "It's Raining Men" and "We Are Family." I loved those disco hits, but I knew enough to keep this a secret in front of other guys. My sisters were also into Rick Springfield. Every day after school, I'd watch *General Hospital* with them to see if Rick was finally going to make some sharin'-the-night-together magic with Bobbie Spencer. One night, Mom and Dad took Tracey and her friends to see Rick Springfield at the Providence Civic Center. On the way out of the parking lot, they got behind a bus that everybody agreed *had* to be Rick Springfield's tour bus. My dad tailed the bus all the way up I-95 to Boston, with four girls screaming in the backseat. They lost him on the Southeast Expressway, right near the Chinatown exit, but Dad drove around to all the downtown hotels so the girls could barge into the lobbies and ask for Mr. Springfield. To this day, Tracey's computer password is MUS-134, Rick's license plate.

I always envied my friends who had older siblings who could guide them through the teenage wasteland. They got a head start. My next-door neighbor Jeff had an older brother, Barry, and an older sister, Susan. I would often sit in the tree in our front yard and breathe in their aura. Every weekend, Barry wore his T-shirt with the cover of Boston's first album, and washed his Trans Am in the driveway while cranking "Peace of Mind." He had a basement room with black lightbulbs, guitars, and a piranha. Some afternoons, he'd let us watch the piranha eat goldfish. He also had a girlfriend named Nancy, who he wouldn't let us watch at all.

Susan was a real seventies girl, blond feathered hair and all, one braid dangling down the side of her face. Her CB-radio handle was Whammer Jammer, after a J. Geils Band song. Once

I was in the tree while she was on the porch with a boy. I was hoping she didn't see me, but she came over to talk. She said, "You won't tell my mom I was smoking, will you?" I said, Of course not. She kissed me on the cheek and said, "You're a doll." She was more than a woman to me.

Every day Susan came home after school and followed the same ritual: She opened her bedroom window and played one or both of her favorite albums, Fleetwood Mac's *Rumours* (side two only) and Boz Scaggs's *Silk Degrees* (side one only). Sometimes, she would just play her favorite songs. She would play Boz Scaggs's "Georgia" for hours, lifting the needle over and over. If Susan wasn't in the mood for "Georgia," she would play the second half of Fleetwood Mac's "The Chain," starting with the bass solo and then going into the "Chaaa-yaaay-yaaain!" chant. I would sit in my tree, gazing up at Susan's window and trying to imagine her intense communion with the music and what it must feel like inside her soul at such moments.

When you're a little kid, you're fascinated by the mystery of what the big kids do, and for me these mysteries were associated with music. The music I loved kept scaring the bejeezus out of me, with the nebulous concepts of "sex" and "drugs." I'd sit in the basement with Eddie and Jimmy Durfer, listening to records like Meat Loaf's *Bat out of Hell* or Kiss's *Alive II*, trying to figure out the plots. The music was full of danger. Every note evoked the terror of the don't-take-drugs paperbacks I'd read at school, like *Go Ask Alice* ("Dear diary, the squirrels are eating my face again") or *That Was Then, This Is Now* ("The colors screamed at me! Purple screamed loudest!"). At school, we studied Rush's *2112* and *Lord of the Rings*. In the cafeteria, I looked anxiously at my chocolate milk and recalled how Alice got dosed at the sleep-over party. Was somebody playing "button, button, who's got the button" with our lunches? Would my teacher do such a thing? Why not? She was into *Lord of the Rings*. I was just one chocolate-milk mustache away from slipping into a hellhole of bare feet and crash pads and diary entries like "another day, another blowjob" until my inevitable fatal pot overdose.

But I couldn't wait for the eighth-grade dance—this was the culmination of my years of obsession with rockness. I spent days sweating over those dance tapes.

"Hey, I like this one," my mom said. "We will, we will rock you! That's a catchy song!"

I erased "We Will Rock You."

The night of the dance, the whole class gathered in Strauss Hall. The girls looked very cool over on their side of the room, a swirl of velour and Love's Baby Soft. The boys did not look so cool. Every time a rocking song came on, the girls would sit down. It was enough to make you doubt their commitment to rockness. When the boys busted out the air guitar, the girls parked the Calvin Klein labels on their jeans firmly on the bench. In fact, the harder the boys rocked, the farther away the girls drifted. That night, I learned the hard way: If the girls keep dancing, everybody's happy. If the girls don't dance, *nobody's* happy.

The girls got hot for "Pop Muzik" and "Heart of Glass" and "Bad Girls." The boys stood around and waited for rock anthems so we could untuck our shirts and chant the lyrics to "Hot Blooded," which by some strange coincidence were the same as the title. But all the majesty of rock could not impress these girls; it failed to move their stony hearts despite the cathedral-like grandeur of Tom Scholz's guitar solo in the second movement of Boston's "Don't Look Back." Asking a classmate to dance was scary enough when the song was a girl-pleaser. But when the song involved acoustic guitars and elaborate metaphors about bustles in hedgerows? Out of the question! Girls did not care whether a dance tape had the live version of "Carry On Wayward Son" or the studio version. In fact, they did not want to hear "Carry On Wayward Son" at all. What was wrong with these people?

It was a painful night, but I got the message: Let the dancing girls dance. That's the one ironclad rule of pop muzik, whether in New York, London, Paris, or Munich, and I'm just lucky I learned it so early. I had always been taught to fear disco, and to fear the disco inside me. But by the second verse of "Bad Girls," it was obvious everything I knew was wrong. "Toot toot, beep beep" was meaningful on a much deeper level than I could have fathomed.

For me, this was a humbling lesson, as well as my introduction to the principle of "bitch power," as first elucidated by the great twentieth-century philosopher Rick James. Bitch power

blew my mind. Rick explained it all in an issue of *Creem* magazine that I carried around in my backpack. According to Rick
James:

> It's this kind of syndrome—where if a guy sees his
> girlfriend likin' somebody, that's called 'bitch power.'
> Like Elvis Presley was hated by men, *hated*, 'cause he
> had bitch power. Teddy Pendergrass has bitch power.
> I just found out that *I* have a little bitch power. But
> beyond bitch power, I have something else, that men
> *like*—and that's the *truth*, and the down-to-earth shit,
> OK? So men don't mind bringin' their women to see
> me, 'cause I have bitch power but it's in another way.

If Rick is to be trusted—and he always is—bitch power is the
juice, the sweat, the blood that keeps pop music going. Rick
James helped me understand the lesson of the eighth-grade
dance: Bitch power rules the world. If the girls don't like the
music, they sit down and stop the show. You gotta have a crowd
if you wanna have a show. And the girls *are* the show. We're talking absolute monarchy, with no rules of succession. Bitch
power. She must be obeyed. She must be feared.

As a thirteen-year-old boy, I had plenty of reasons to fear
bitch power. But when she came knocking, I had no choice. I
bowed and worshiped. Toot toot. Beep beep. But I have to
admit, I have no regrets about including the live version of

Aerosmith's "Dream On." I picked the song because it was a slow dance, but I picked the live version because Steven Tyler screams the word "motherfucker" in the second verse ("all the things you do, motherfucker, come back to yooouuuuu!"), and that was just *so* cool. For that one line, I cranked the volume up into the red, hoping it would rile the chaperoning math teachers, not realizing that they were way too stoned to notice. I also knew that "Dream On" came on right after "Off the Wall," and I decided to exploit this inside knowledge. I innocently chose that moment to ask the beautiful Sarah Farrah Field Hockey to dance, before she or anybody else realized it was Aerosmith slow-dance time. This is one of the most daring things I did in my entire life. But I paid the price. As I held loosely to the long-pined-for waistline of Sarah Farrah Field Hockey and frantically tried to hide my boner, my friends were making faces at me behind her back, trying to make me giggle. While Steven Tyler was dreaming on until his dreams came true, Sarah Farrah Field Hockey was smirking, "What's so funny?" The horror. The horror.

tape 635

JUNE 1980

A SIDE ONE DATE/TIME	**B** SIDE TWO DATE/TIME
Cheap Trick: "Surrender"	• Cheap Trick: "Ain't That a Shame"
Boz Scaggs: "Lowdown"	• Cheap Trick: "Clock Strikes Ten"
ELO: "Turn to Stone"	• The Guess Who: "American Woman"
ELO: "Sweet Talkin' Woman"	• Supertramp: "The Logical Song"
Steely Dan: "Reelin' in the Years"	• Led Zeppelin: "Stairway to Heaven"
The Cars: "Just What I Needed"	• Rolling Stones: "Jumpin' Jack Flash"
The Eagles: "Life in the Fast Lane"	• Rickie Lee Jones: "Chuck E.'s in Love"
Rolling Stones: "Satisfaction"	• Gerry Rafferty: "Get It Right Next
Lynyrd Skynyrd: "Free Bird"	• Time"
Queen: "Bohemian Rhapsody"	• The Knack: "My Sharona"
Fleetwood Mac: "Go Your Own Way"	• J. Geils Band: "Where Did Our Love Go"
	• Cheap Trick: "Dream Police"
	• Nick Lowe: "Crackin' Up"
	• Squeeze: "Cool for Cats"

Camp Don Bosco in East Barrington, New Hampshire, was a Catholic summer camp for boys aged eight to fifteen, run by priests and brothers of the Salesian Order. I was a camper there in the summers of 1980 and 1981. It was in the middle of a pine forest four hours north of Boston, with a lake and grassy dells, far from any other human dwelling.

St. John Bosco (1815–1888) was an Italian priest, canonized in 1934, who founded the Salesian Order to bring the gospel to destitute boys.

Almost all the campers were Italian kids from East Boston who also attended Salesian vocational schools. Others, including me, were from the suburbs or other parts of New England. A tiny minority were local country boys who kept to themselves. There were three cabins: St. Pat's for little kids; Savio for medium kids; Magone for us big kids.

Brother Larry, in charge of Magone, was a gentle soul, always willing to discuss religious problems at the drop of a hat. He walked around for an hour every night after lights-out to make sure nobody was committing self-pollution. He taught me to shoot a rifle; I still have a couple of NRA "Advanced Marksman" certificates in my parents' attic.

Brother Jim was a biker who'd done time. He was in charge of Savio cabin, which meant scaring the shit out of any Magone kids who tried to pick on Savio kids. There was a rumor he had a switchblade on him.

Brother Jim loved to talk about how Jesus wasn't a pussy.

"You see the guy crucified up there?" he yelled. "You see him? Are his hands closed? NO! Is he making a fist? NO! What does that mean to you?"

We sat there, cowering.

"It means something to *me*."

More cowering.

"It means he could have just gotten down off the cross

anytime he liked, and come down and WASTED all those Roman gladiator motherfuckers. But he kept his hands OPEN! He let it go! For YOU! And you sit here and look at that dead guy up there and *you don't even notice!*"

Brother Jim was seriously cool.

Brother Dave, the folksinger, wore a Jesus beard and sandals. At Mass, he strummed an acoustic guitar and sang his original compositions, like "Dare to Be Different." There was a vague sense that the other brothers did not fully accept him as an equal.

Brother Al was a jovial Polish guy with a Gabe Kaplan mustache. He once literally washed out a kid's mouth with soap. I saw it happen. Crandall took the Lord's name in vain, and Brother Al flew off the handle and dragged him to the sink at the back of the cabin with a bar of Irish Spring.

Salesians have their own icons and folklore—when they get mad, they yell, "Mother Cabrini!" They were always telling magical tales about Don Bosco, who had visions, and St. Dominic Savio, a fifteen-year-old who died of consumption because he was sleeping naked to catch cold and do penance for his sins. Sex and death and Italian mystagogy were in the air!

There was a stigma against admitting you were trained as an altar boy, because it meant admitting you dressed up in a cassock and surplice. I was the only kid at Camp Don Bosco who would admit he was an altar boy back home, so I served two Masses a day all summer. But I loved the cassock and surplice, ringing the bells, lighting the candles—it was like being a glam-rock roadie for God. It might have earned me the contempt of my fellow campers, but it gave me a chance to bond with Sister Veronica and Sister Catherine, the nuns who took care of the chapel. While the other guys were riding horses or shooting hoops, I was working the cassock, swishing the surplice. Back home, my favorite part of Mass was during communion, when I'd stand at the rail and hold a little gold platter under people's chins. The pretty girls would line up for communion (*I confess to Almighty God*). They'd kneel (*and to you my brothers and sisters*), cast their eyes demurely down (*I have sinned through my own fault*), and stick out their tongues (*in my thoughts and in my words*). Their tongues would shine, reflected in the gold platter, and since the wafer was dry, the girls would maybe lick their lips (*and I ask Blessed Mary ever virgin, all the angels and saints, and you my brothers and sisters*) before they swallowed (*to pray for me to the Lord our God*). It was all I could do not to pass out.

I was a little psycho about religion. My teen malaise found a language in the blood and glory of Catholic angst. All kids lead a secret double life, and this was mine. I slept with Thomas a Kempis's *Imitation of Christ* under my pillow. I idolized St. Rose of Lima, who rubbed raw pepper on her face so her beauty would not be a temptation to the chastity of others. I devoted myself to mastering the underground occult lore of the Catholic hardcore—Butler's *Lives of the Saints* and Augustine and T-Money Aquinas—the way other kids would devote themselves to D&D or the

Foundation trilogy. My moral compass was shaped mainly by the Second Vatican Council, plus the episode of *Welcome Back, Kotter* where Arnold Horshack refuses to dissect a frog.

One spring, I even decided to give up evil music for Lent. It meant seven weeks of listening to the radio and wondering which songs were evil and which songs were just *about* evil. I decided the Stones' "Sympathy for the Devil" was okay because it was anti-devil, but the Grateful Dead's "Friend of the Devil" was soft on Satan. I gave myself permission to keep cranking Jim Carroll's "People Who Died" because it was so saturated with evil that it amounted to a critique of evil, but not Lou Reed's "Walk on the Wild Side," which was just plain evil. I made a specially edited tape of *London Calling* to omit the nun-fucking. These theological judgments made my head hurt, and I was relieved when Lent was over. On Easter morning, I treated myself to "Walk on the Wild Side."

My rock heroes were wild-side jaywalkers like Lou Reed, Bob Dylan, and David Bowie, guys who smirked at heartbreak through their inch-thick steel shades. They gave me the hope that teenage outcasts could grow up to be something besides corpses or cartoons. Jesus was my Major Tom. He said, "My kingdom is not of this world." So did Bowie. It tapped into the whole Catholic idea of creating your own saints, finding icons of divinity in the mundane. As a religion, Bowieism didn't seem so different from Catholicism—the hemlines were just a little higher. Of course, when Madonna hit, she was a one-woman

Vatican 3, but at this point I had all the rock-star saints I could handle.

At Camp Don Bosco, there were Bibles all over the place, mostly 1970s hippie versions like *Good News for Modern Man*. They had groovy titles like *The Word* or *The Way*, and translated the Bible into "contemporary English," which meant Saul yelling at Jonathan, "You son of a bitch!" (I Samuel 20:30). Awesome! The King James version gave this verse as "Thou son of the perverse rebellious woman," which was bogus in comparison. Maybe these translations went a bit far. I recall one of the Bibles translating the inscription over the cross, "INRI" (Iesus Nazaremus Rex Iudaeorum), as "SSDD" (Same Shit Different Day), and another describing the Last Supper—the night before Jesus' death, a death he freely accepted—where Jesus breaks the bread, gives it to his disciples, and says, "It's better to burn out than fade away," but these memories could be deceptive.

At Camp Don Bosco, I met another camper who was a Beatles freak, which was like finding gold. Aldo Rettagliatti and I spent hours debating the Paul-is-dead clues and *Abbey Road* (his favorite) vs. the *White Album* (mine). Since we were out in the middle of the woods, with no radio and a load of religious tracts around, we soon got into some Catholic-mystic Beatle talk. We elaborated ideas about the way "Revolution 9" rewrote chapter nine of the Book of Revelation. We took our theory to Brother Larry, but he assured us that the Book of Revelation was too hard for us to interpret, and besides, Jesus didn't write it, and anyway, everything after *Sgt. Pepper* was crap.

Socially, the campers split into three groups: tough guys, wise guys, and pussies. The pussies spent the summer in constant danger from the tough guys, while the wise guys tried to *nyuk-nyuk-nyuk* their way out of violent situations, mostly by making fun of the pussies. I was a wise guy, except when my inner pussy would slip out from under my cassock and surplice.

Camp Don Bosco was my first male peer group, and it was a shock to learn that boys were, in fact, dipshits. The mystery I'd always thought surrounded tough guys just disappeared. Here's an actual conversation I heard on the picnic tables outside the canteen that summer:

CRANDALL: *So, how many times have you done it with her?*
COLANTINO: *None. She's a virgin bitch.*
CRANDALL: *Virgins are the worst kind! It takes so long to get it!*
COLANTINO: *But virgins are the best kind when you do get it.*
CRANDALL: *But it takes so long!*

Crandall was a fourteen-year-old dork, and sounded like a real idiot bragging about sex, but he was in with the tough guys because his best friend was ringleader Steve Doherty, a sociopathic Scott Baio look-alike. The only kid allowed to give Crandall shit was Doherty's little brother, who was in St. Pat's. Spaz was a tiny kid from Dorchester who lost more fights than he won, but he was crazy and would fight *anybody*, so he got the respect normally reserved for the tough guys who spent their leisure time kicking the shit out of Spaz. Spaz wore a scapular around his neck, a string of holy medallions that consecrated him to Mary. Supposedly, if you die wearing one, you go straight to heaven. But one night, Brother Al told us all a cautionary tale about a man who thought he could get away with his sinful ways because he wore the scapular. "He led a very immoral life," Brother Al told us, pacing the floor after lights-out. "He did everything." After he died in a car crash, the police found his scapular . . . dangling from a nearby tree!

Mike McGrath was the only tough guy who took a liking to me, and without him, I wouldn't have lasted a week at Camp Bosco. Mike was from my parish, St. Mary's, and we'd been confirmed together. His big brother, called "Urko" after some evil gorilla on the *Planet of the Apes* TV series, was one of Milton's scariest delinquents. Mike was just a joke back home, but at camp he told everybody he was "Big Mac," and I didn't blow his cover, so he looked out for me. ("Ape shall never kill ape.")

Everybody complained that Camp Don Bosco was too far from Boston to pick up our beloved WCOZ. The only radio we got was a local country station, which only Brother Al could stomach. We all missed WCOZ on Sunday nights, which was when the Dr. Demento show aired. But instead of radio, we had Bubba Colantino's "master blaster" boombox and five tapes in heavy cranktation. Our two biggest albums were "2" and "Zeppelin," normally listed in reference works as *Led Zeppelin II* and *Led Zeppelin IV*. Some people call the latter "Zoso," but I never heard it called that at Camp Don Bosco. Damone in *Fast Times* calls it *Led Zeppelin Four*. The Columbia House Record and Tape Club ads listed it as *Runes*. But the guys at camp just said, "Put the Zeppelin on." (A "Zeppelin" was also a kind of bong that looked like a thermos and held two roaches and filled up with enough smoke to choke an elephant.) When Steve Doherty said, "Put on two," he meant the album with "Whole Lotta Love." The three other albums we blasted all summer were *Hi Infidelity*, *Crimes of Passion*, and *Back in Black*—Brother Larry approved of the theology of "Hells Bells."

The guy with the most Zeppelin tapes was Mullen, the junior counselor in charge of St. Pat's. I knew him from my grandparents' parish, St. Andrew's in Forest Hills. Mullen shaved his head and never said a word. There was a story going around that some lady had offered him a hundred bucks to beat up her son all summer, to toughen the boy up, but that Mullen had turned her down. Nonetheless, all the Magone guys were too scared to touch any St. Pat's kids because that was Mullen's cabin. I didn't understand the tough guys—I thought the whole point was to be tough so you wouldn't have to be afraid, but it seemed to me that the tough guys were constantly watching for the guys who were just a little tougher. They were busier being scared than I was. It was like *Planet of the Apes*, and I knew I was a chimpanzee who would never pass for a gorilla.

But there's one memory I have about Steve Doherty that I still wonder about from time to time. We were all standing around the lake after dinner one night, with AC/DC on the box, when Doherty said, "I hate disco people—you know, disco *pants*. But there are some disco *songs*, you know, like 'Funky-town,' that rock." Believe me, nobody else could've talked that shit and made it back to the cabin alive. Maybe Doherty was just screwing with us, seeing what he could get away with. ("Ape has killed ape!") Or maybe he really dug "Funkytown." I'll never know, because we all just nodded and said, "Uh-huh."

love makes me do foolish things

A SIDE ONE DATE/TIME	B SIDE TWO DATE/TIME
R.E.M.: "It's The End of the World as We Know It (And I Feel Fine)"	Martha & the Vandellas: "Love (Makes Me Do Foolish Things)"
Kajagoogoo: "Too Shy"	Aretha Franklin: "Don't Play That Song"
Thelonious Monk: "Memories of You"	Aretha Franklin: "Day Dreaming"
ABC: "That Was Then But This Is Now"	Aretha Franklin: "Angel"
Eric Carmen: "She Did It"	Aretha Franklin: "Until You Come Back to Me"
Yaz: "Nobody's Diary"	Alex Chilton: "Take It Off"
Magazine: "Shot by Both Sides"	Lou Reed: "Bottoming Out"
Jimi Hendrix: "Little Wing"	Johnny Thunders: "It's Not Enough"
Jimi Hendrix: "Bold as Love"	Baby Astronauts: "Lost at Your Party"
The Beatles: "What You're Doing"	The Verlaines: "Death and the Maiden"
The Beatles: "Yes It Is"	The Flying Lizards: "Sex Machine"
The Dogmatics: "Cry Myself to Sleep"	

This was my very first breakup tape, slapped together in the aftermath of my very first breakup. I was twenty-one. My social skills had not advanced all that much since my *Roller Boogie* days, I'm sad to say. I was just one of those graves that pretty girls make. I wore black every day, and grooved to the morose strains of Lou Reed and Richard Thompson and Tom Verlaine. I was a senior at Yale, plugged in to my Walkman, still hiding from the world most of the time. In fact, until I met my first girlfriend, Maria, I was a safe bet to graduate from college without ever having kissed a woman, a fate spared me only when Maria launched a tenacious attack on my innocence not unlike the one led by Charles Bronson in the 1970s TV movie *Raid on Entebbe*.

It was a spring romance that lasted, blissfully, all summer long. Maria was obsessed with R.E.M. and Sonic Youth; she also taught me to wear Converse high-tops, smoked and drank, and did all kinds of wild shit that was new to me. We spent the summer sitting in her room, under her Michael Stipe posters, listening to R.E.M. bootlegs. I DJ'd the all-night radio show on WYBC, so Maria would always call me on the air at 4 A.M. to request the Modern Lovers' "Hospital."

When we broke up, I was devastated. I made myself this breakup tape as a sound track for my afternoon walks through the city. It includes lots of sad guitar dudes and soul singers, especially Martha and the Vandellas, sobbing their way through "Love (Makes Me Do Foolish Things)." The opening drums of that lost Motown gem still make me gasp, ushering me into Martha's lonely room, where she doesn't even have any Vandellas to keep her company, just weepy piano and strings and drums. Martha sits there on the edge of her bed, praying to hear that knock on her door, except she knows she will never hear that knock . . . no *more*! I would rewind and play that song over and over, certain that if I could only hear all the way through Martha's voice to the core of her soul I, too, could suffer gorgeously enough to be one of her Vandellas.

Before I met Maria, I was your basic craven hermit. I spent most of my time in my room, in love with my walls, hiding out from the world with my fanzines and my records. I thought I was happier that way. I had developed these monastic habits to protect myself from something, probably, but whatever it was, the monastic habits had turned into the bigger problem. In my headphones, I led a life of romance and incident and intrigue, none of which had anything to do with the world outside my Walkman. I was an English major, obsessed with Oscar Wilde and Walter Pater and Algernon Swinburne, thrilling to the exploits of my decadent aesthete poet idols, even though my only experience with decadence was reading about it.

My chick friends were always trying to find girls for me. They were my mentors in girl vanity, and after growing up with three sisters, I was a more than capable student. My chick friends got tired of their boyfriends pretty fast, but they didn't get tired of me; I nursed them through romantic crises and answered their tearful late-night calls. I knew the hell they wreaked on their boyfriends, and I thought it was funny—man, their boyfriends were suckers. I was too smart for such things. I lived by the code of Emersonian self-reliance. "Leave your theory, as Joseph his coat in the hand of the harlot, and flee," Emerson thundered. "If any one imagines that this law is lax, let him keep its commandment one day."

I was young, idealistic, and reluctant to learn any of the ways of the world, even when it would have been to my advantage to do so. I was wasted, not on drugs, but on something possibly worse. I read an aphorism of Nietzsche's, in which he says, "The man who despises himself still respects himself as one who despises." I laughed and said, Totally. That describes everybody I know, except me. It was time for a change.

But how do you start getting out of your room? I was reading a poem by my idol, Wallace Stevens, in which he said, "The self is a cloister of remembered sounds." My first response was, Yesss! How did he know that? It's like he's reading my mind. But my second response was, I need some new sounds to remember. I've been stuck in my little isolation chamber for so long I'm spinning through the same sounds I've been hearing in my head all my life. If I go on this way, I'll get old too fast, without remembering any more sounds than I already know now. The only one who remembers any of my sounds is me. How do you turn down the volume on your personal-drama earphones and learn how to listen to other people? How do you jump off one moving train, marked Yourself, and jump onto a train moving in the opposite direction, marked Everybody Else? I loved a Modern Lovers song called, "Don't Let Our Youth Go to Waste," and I didn't want to waste mine.

I felt like I was strong enough for a girl, but made for a woman. Yet I had no idea how to start looking to find this woman. Fortunately, she was looking for me.

Maria was a cool, punk-rock girl from Georgia who worked

at the Waldenbooks in the Chapel Square Mall. She dyed her hair red and played bass in a hardcore band, the Uncalled Four. She'd dropped out of high school and taken the bus to New Haven to be with a boy. They broke up as soon as she arrived, but she stayed around town and got a job. One night, she spotted me at a hardcore show and smelled blood. She invited me over to her place. The first things I noticed were the Michael Stipe poster on the wall, her boombox, and loads of tapes. Then I noticed that she had no furniture except a mattress on the floor. You know the Beatles song where the girl invites John to sit down, except she doesn't have a chair? This girl didn't even have a *rug*. She put on a tape from her vast collection of R.E.M. bootlegs, a rehearsal tape from 1982. Michael Stipe started to sing "The Lion Sleeps Tonight." The room began to spin.

I couldn't believe she liked me. I couldn't believe how much I liked her. She told me I looked like Dr. Robert from the Blow Monkeys. No girl ever told me I looked like *anything* before. In the evenings, I would get off work at the library and take the bus up Whalley Avenue to her house, where we'd order pizza and watch MTV. It was a great summer for bittersweet songs about the pangs of first love: Lou Gramm's "Midnight Blue," Simply Red's "The Right Thing," Eddie Money's "Endless Nights," Janet Jackson's "Let's Wait Awhile," Mötley Crüe's "Too Young to Fall in Love," Sheila E.'s "Koo Koo," Poison's "Talk Dirty to Me."

It was the first time I had ever been in love. Suddenly, I felt like part of the world. I had never met a southern girl before, so Maria was full of surprises: She baked pies, she fried catfish, she pronounced "umbrella" funny, she called me "baby" totally unironically. I wondered, Where have southern girls been all my life? She was also an avid shoplifter. She told me it was easy—the managers at chain stores were not allowed to interfere with shoplifters because the corporate bosses were afraid of lawsuits, so she could walk right through the scanners with her arms full of goodies and they wouldn't do a thing to stop her. All my female friends assured me this was a lie. Maria invited me to watch her shoplift but I was too nervous to make a good wheelman.

She'd keep me on the phone for hours during my all-night radio shows, and I would play songs for her, improvising a mix tape on the air. If anybody else was listening, which I doubt, they probably had no idea what was going on. Maybe indie rock circa '87 was not the most romantic music—boys in basements screaming for other boys in basements—and yet there was plenty of romance to be heard in that, if you were listening. And we were. I had been to lots of rock shows, but I had never held hands at one. Maria used to play me R.E.M.'s live version of "All I Have to Do Is Dream," recorded the same day she got off the bus in New Haven. We listened to Prince's *Sign 'O' the Times*. (Everybody's favorite Prince album must be the first one they heard while actually making out.) I made her a tape called *Ciccone Island Baby*. She made me a tape called *Jumpin' Sylvia Plath, It's a Gas Gas Gas*. It was love, obviously.

Maria was a door-slammer, big on stomping out of rooms and expecting me to follow. I was new at this boyfriend stuff, so

I didn't question her way of doing things. Her roommate hated me (I used too many paper towels), and they had screaming fights about me, which was hot. But things started to wobble around the time R.E.M. put out a truly wretched album called *Document*, the one that made her reconsider whether she could continue to worship Michael Stipe. I blamed R.E.M. for not saving us by making a better record. That, I realize now, was unfair.

It was young. It was true. It lasted about six months. October first was the end of the world as I knew it. She called to say it was over. Well, not in those words—what she said was, "I'm fed up to my back teeth with you." I sat on my bed and looked out at the city lights. My clock radio was playing Elton John's "Someone Saved My Life Tonight." I realized I would never get to put this song on a tape for Maria, and my face began to crumple. She gave me a farewell gift, a 1988 Bon Jovi calendar shoplifted from Sam Goody, which was a nice gesture, but that was the end. I felt sad when her friends stopped saying hi to me at rock shows, but I didn't realize that's just the way it rolls. I loathed myself for secretly wishing I'd taped her records before she ditched me.

At least I had Martha and the Vandellas to guide me through the experience. They didn't have any good news, but they sure didn't lie. Love makes me do foolish things. I was lucky to learn early.

big star: for renée

OCTOBER 1989

A SIDE ONE DATE/TIME	B SIDE TWO DATE/TIME
Big Star: Sister Lovers	• Big Star: Radio City
plus	• plus
The Bats: "Sir Queen"	• Lucinda Williams: "I Just Wanted to See
Velvet Underground: "Radio Ad"	• You So Bad"
	• The Raincoats: "Only Loved at Night"
	• Marti Jones: "Lonely Is (as Lonely
	• Does)"
	•
	•
	•

As far as mix tapes go, Big Star: For Renée is totally unimaginative. It's basically just one complete album on each side of a tape. But this is the tape that changed everything. Everything in my life comes directly from this Maxell XLII crush tape, made on October 10, 1989, for Renée.

Renée and I met at a bar called the Eastern Standard in Charlottesville, Virginia. I had just moved there to study English in grad school. Renée was a fiction writer in the MFA program. I was sitting with my poet friend Chris at a table in the back when

I fell under the spell of Renée's bourbon-baked voice. The bartender put on Big Star's *Radio City*. Renée was the only other person in the room who perked up. We started talking about how much we loved Big Star. It turned out we had the same favorite Big Star song—the acoustic ballad "Thirteen." She'd never heard their third album, *Sister Lovers*. So, naturally, I told her the same thing I'd told every other woman I'd ever fallen for: "I'll make you a tape!"

As Renée left the bar, I asked my friend, "What was that girl's name again?"

"Renée."

"She's really beautiful."

"Uh-huh. And there's her boyfriend."

The boyfriend's name was Jimm, and he really did spell his name with two M's—a dealbreaker if I ever heard one. Renée had actually just broken up with the guy that night, but I didn't know that yet. So I just cursed my luck, and crushed out on her from afar. I memorized her teaching schedule and hung around the English department whenever she had office hours, hoping to run into her in the hallway. I wrote poems about her. I made her this tape and slipped it into her mailbox. I just taped my two favorite Big Star albums and filled up the spaces at the end of the tape with other songs I liked, hoping it would impress her. How cool was this girl? She was an Appalachian country girl from southwestern Virginia. She had big, curly brown hair, little round glasses, and a girlish drawl. I just knew her favorite Go-Go was Jane Wiedlin.

One Saturday night we met at a party and danced to a few B-52's songs. Like all southern girls, Renée had an intense relationship with the first three B-52's albums. "All girls are either Kate girls or Cindy girls," she told me. "Like how boys are either Beatles or Stones boys. You like them both, but there's only one who's totally yours." Her B-52 idol was Kate, the brunette with the auburn melancholy in her voice. I wanted to stay all night and keep talking to Renée about the B-52's, but my ride wanted to go early. So I left her stranded and went home to pace up and down the parking lot outside the subdivision, shivering in the cold with my Walkman, listening to Prince's "Little Red Corvette." The ache in his voice summed up my mood, as he sang about a girl driving right past him, the kind of car that doesn't pass you every day.

Renée and I ran into each other again when the poet John Ashbery came to town for a reading. He was one of my idols, the man who wrote *The Double Dream of Spring*. I got to meet him after the reading, but I blew it. A bunch of us were hovering around, trying to think of clever things to say. He'd just read his poem "The Songs We Know Best" and was explaining that he'd written it to go with the melody of Peaches & Herb's "Reunited" because the song was all over the radio and he couldn't get the tune out of his head. So I asked if he was a fan of Wham!'s "Last Christmas," which of course has the same melody as "Reunited." He smiled graciously and said no, he wasn't, but that he liked George Michael. Then he went back to saying nothing at all and my friends were furious and I was mortified

and I will go to my grave wondering why I spent my one moment in the presence of this great man discussing Wham! (and
not even a *good* Wham! song), but I guess that's the double
dream of dipshit I am.

Afterward I stood at the bar, drowning my sorrows. Renée
came up to kick my shins and bum a cigarette. She mentioned
that her birthday was coming up in a few days. As always, there
were a few other boys from her fan club hovering around, so we
all went out for a late-night tour of Charlottesville's cheaper
drinking establishments. I squeezed into a booth next to her
and we talked about music. She told me you can sing the *Beverly
Hillbillies* theme to the tune of R.E.M.'s "Talk About the Passion." That was it, basically; as soon as she started to sing "Talk
About the Clampetts," any thought I had of not falling in love
with her went down in some serious *Towering Inferno* flames. It
was over. I was over.

We hung out again the next night—Renée showed up with
another gang of suitor boys, all giving her puppy-dog looks, but
I wasn't too worried about outlasting them. Joe passed out
around midnight. Paul staggered out a few minutes later. Steve's
offer to help walk Renée home lasted as long as it took for him
to smash into the wall twice on his way down the stairs. I was
the last man standing. Renée led me to her place, a couple of
miles away. It was so dark I couldn't see her at all while we
walked; I just followed her voice. I spent the night on her couch,
sleeping under a huge portrait of her painted by some sweet
indie-rock boy back in Roanoke. I was a little sad about being on

the couch, but I was going for the long bomb. Her incredibly annoying cat, Molly, kept jumping on my face all night. I woke up at dawn and lay there drowsing, feeling a little less lonely than I had the morning before, waiting for this girl to make some noise.

Renée had Saturday errands to run, and I invited myself along to keep her company. We drove all around Charlottesville in the afternoon sun. We listened to a mix tape another guy had made her, back in Roanoke. It had some lame indie rock, some decent indie rock, and one really great song: Flatt & Scruggs doing their bluegrass version of "Ode to Billie Joe." She told me she'd thrown a Billie Joe party that summer. "I had it on the third of June," she crowed. "You know, the day the song takes place. I served all the food they eat in the song: black-eyed peas, biscuits, apple pie."

We couldn't think of anything else to talk about, so we just drove in silence until she dropped me off at my place. I spent the rest of the day making a birthday tape for her, mostly Senegalese acoustic music by Baaba Maal and Mansour Seck, just in case she smoked pot. I started to add Bob Dylan's "I Want You," but then thought better of it. Instead, I added Scrawl's "Breaker Breaker," to show off my affinity with feminist trucker punk songs, and the Neville Brothers, to make her think maybe *I* smoked pot.

We met up at a dive called the Garrett on Monday, the night before her birthday. It was not a romantic bar—the carpet was so pot-soaked you got a buzz walking to the bathroom—but it offered privacy, cheap liquor, a cigarette machine that was easy to tilt, and pool tables to distract pain-in-the-ass innocent bystanders. I'd spent the day writing a sonnet sequence for her. I'm not sure what I was thinking—I mean, I used the word "catachresis" in the first line. But I was certain my prosodic ingenuity would melt her heart for good. I used one of my favorite rhyme schemes—stolen from the James Merrill poem "The Octopus," though he'd stolen it himself, from W. H. Auden's *The Sea and the Mirror*—rhyming the first syllable of a trochee with the final syllable in the next line. How could she resist?

At midnight, I gave her the poems.

"What's going on?" she asked.

"Well, the last word in the first line is a trochee, and it rhymes with the end of the next line. So 'catachresis' rhymes with 'fleece.'"

"No, what's going *on*?"

"In a catachresis?"

"No. What are you talking about?"

"Uh . . . I have a big crush on you."

"*Oooooh*," she said. She smiled and let the pages drop on the table. She relaxed in front of my eyes. "So how did it start?"

"Well, I think you're really beautiful."

She relaxed a lot more—in fact, her face changed shape a little, got a little more round, as if her jaw had unclenched. I didn't know whether that was a good sign or not, but I couldn't shut up yet.

"I always thought so. Right away, when I saw you."

"The amazing black dress," she nodded. "I was wearing that when I met you. There's, uh, a lot of *me* in that dress. My Fuck the Hostess dress. It's a real 'drop to your knees and say amen' dress."

"I noticed. It's gotten worse since then."

"I know." She lit one of my Dunhills. I had never seen her so comfortable. "I was on the phone with my friend Merit tonight, and she was like, Does Rob like you? And I said, I don't know, he made me a tape and he didn't call and then we danced together and then he left and called and left a message but didn't call after that. And Merit was like, So, do you like Rob?"

I couldn't believe she was making me do this. "So, do you?"

She smiled. "I don't know. He's not my type, but I really like him." She told me her type was farm boys with broad shoulders, football players. She took her time smoking that cigarette. She still had most of her beer left and she was in no hurry at all. I was too scared to talk, but I was more scared to not talk.

"I don't know what your type is. I don't know what your deal is. I don't even know if you have a boyfriend. I know I like you and I want to be in your life, that's it, and if you have any room for a boyfriend, I would like to be your boyfriend, and if you don't have any room, I would like to be your friend. Any room you have for me in your life is great. If you would like me to start out in one room and move to another, I could do that."

"But you'd rather be a boyfriend than a friend?"

"Given the choice. No, not given the choice. That's what I want."

"Where are you parked?"

"I walked."

"What's a catachresis?"

"A rhetorical inversion of tense, kind of like a transumption. Let's go."

In her car, we listened to Marshall Crenshaw's first album, and when we got to her place, we sat on the couch under that big painting. She was not comfortable anymore; she was really scared. She got up and put on my Big Star mix, then took it off. She put on Marshall Crenshaw again. I went through her shoe-boxes of tapes. This girl was definitely an eighties girl. She had a tape with R.E.M.'s *Murmur* on one side and U2's *War* on the other, another with *The Velvet Underground & Nico* backed with *Moondance*. Uh-oh, she also had a lot of XTC tapes. We'd have to work that out later.

"Oh, Rob," she said. "I'm really scared."

I was scared, too. That was a long, long night. I swear her face changed shape several times. I don't know how this is possible, but it did. Her eyelids got heavier and wider. Her breathing got slower and deeper, and her jaw kept dropping lower, making her whole face bigger. She had a solemn look in her eyes. Around dawn, she said, "I hope I do right by you." I didn't know what she meant, so I didn't say anything. I was wearing my Hüsker Dü T-shirt from the *Warehouse* tour. She was wearing a Bob Jones University sweatshirt. I figured there must be a disturbing story there, but I didn't ask.

Sometimes you lie in a strange room, in a strange person's home, and you feel yourself bending out of shape. Melting, touching something hot, something that warps you in drastic and probably irreversible ways you won't get to take stock of until it's too late. I felt myself just melting in Renée's room that night. I remembered being a kid, standing on the bridge over the Pine Tree Brook, when we would find a wax six-ring holder from a six-pack the older kids had killed. We would touch a match to one corner, hold it over the water, and just watch it drip, drip, drip. We'd watch the circular rings, long before the flame even touched them, curl up or bend over in agony. Six rings of wax, twisting and contorting permanently, doing a spastic death dance like the one Christopher Lee does at the end of *Horror of Dracula*, when the sunlight hits him.

The minutes dripped by, each one totally bending and twisting my shape. We eventually stopped getting up to flip the tape, and just listened to dead air. I could feel serious changes happening to me the longer I stayed in Renée's room. I felt knots untie themselves, knots I didn't know were there. I could already tell there were things happening deep inside me that were irreversible. Is there any scarier word than "irreversible"? It's a hiss of a word, full of side effects and mutilations. Severe tire damage—no backing up. Falling in love with Renée felt that way. I felt strange things going on inside me, and I knew that these weren't things I would recover from. These were changes that were shaping the way things were going to be, and I wouldn't find out how until later. Irreversible. I remember that we discussed *The Towering Inferno* that night, the scene with Steve McQueen, the valiant firefighter, and William Holden, the evil tycoon who owns the hotel. William Holden asks, "How bad is it?" and Steve McQueen answers, "It's a fire, mister. And all fires are bad!" That's the last thing I remember before I fell asleep.

sheena was a man

NOVEMBER 1989

A SIDE ONE DATE/TIME	**B** SIDE TWO DATE/TIME
Young MC: "Bust a Move"	• Big Daddy Kane: "Ain't No Half-
Digital Underground:	• Steppin'"
"Doowutchyalike"	• LL Cool J: "I'm That Type of Guy"
Tone Loc: "Wild Thing"	• The Lady Supreme: "I'm That Type
Roxanne Shante: "Live on Stage"	• of Girl"
Public Enemy: "Fight the Power"	• Kool Moe Dee: "They Want Money"
Kings of Swing: "Stop Jockin' James"	• Roxanne Shante: "Go on Girl"
Tone Loc: "Funky Cold Medina"	• EPMD: "Strictly Business"
Heatwave: "The Groove Line"	• Roxanne Shante: "Have a Nice Day"
Inner City: "Good Life"	•
	•

*R*enée was my hero. Have you ever had a hero? Someone who says, I think it would be a good idea for you to steal a car and set it on fire then drive it off a cliff, and you say, Automatic or standard? That's what Renée was. A lion-hearted take-charge southern gal. It didn't take long for us to get all tangled up in each other's hair.

One day that fall we were driving around in her 1978 Chrysler LeBaron and Gladys Knight's "Midnight Train to Georgia" came on the radio. Renée sang lead, while I sang the Pips' backup routine. She's leavin'! Leavin' on the midnight train! Woo woo! A superstar but he didn't get far! When we got to the final fade-out, with Gladys on board the train and the Pips choo-chooing their goodbyes, Renée cocked an eyebrow and said, "You make a good Pip."

That's all I ever wanted to hear a girl tell me. That's all I ever dreamed of being. Some of us are born Gladys Knights, and some of us are born Pips. I marveled unto my Pip soul how lucky I was to choo-choo and woo-woo behind a real Gladys girl.

Girls take up a lot of room. I had a lot of room for this one. She had more energy than anybody I'd ever met. She was in love with the world. She was warm and loud and impulsive. One day, she announced she had found the guitar of her dreams at a local junk shop. I said, "You don't even play the guitar."

She said, "This is the guitar that's gonna teach me."

We drove up Route 29 and she got the guitar. It was a great big Gibson Les Paul with stickers of the Carter Family and the Go-Gos and Lynyrd Skynyrd plastered all over the case. We drove it home and spent the whole weekend kicking around the house as Renée sat on the couch figuring out how to play her favorite Johnny Cash and George Jones songs.

Unlike me, Renée was not shy; she was a real people-pleaser. She worried way too much what people thought of her, wore her heart on her sleeve, expected too much from people, and got hurt too easily. She kept other people's secrets like a champ, but told her own too fast. She expected the world not to cheat her and was always surprised when it did. She was finishing her MFA in fiction, and was always working on stories and novels. She had more ideas than she had time to finish. She loved to get up early in the morning. She loved to talk about wild things she wanted to do in the future. She'd never gone two weeks without a boyfriend since she was fifteen. (Two weeks? I could do a year standing on my head.) Before she met me, her wish list for the next boyfriend had contained three items: older than her (I failed that one), rural (that one, too), and no facial hair (I would have needed six months' notice to slap an acceptable sideburn together).

I often took the bus to her apartment, where we drank bourbon and ginger ale, listened to the music we wanted to impress each other with, which eventually turned into listening to the music we actually liked. She was particular about her bourbon, winced if I forgot to put the ice cubes in before I poured. She'd hiss, "Don't bruise the bourbon!"

She was the first person on either side of her family to go to college, and she held herself to insanely high standards. She worried a lot about whether she was good enough. It was surprising to see how relieved she seemed whenever I told her how amazing she was. I wanted her to feel strong and free. She was beautiful when she was free.

She could play a little piano, mostly hymns that she learned to play for her grandfather. They were tight. When he came home from the mine, she would rub lotion into his blackened hands. When he was on the dialysis machine, she would sit next to him and feed him Pringles. She had some of the scrip they used to pay miners in, instead of cash, to keep them in debt to the mining company. Her grandfather, like mine, worshiped FDR.

Sometimes she would say romantic things like, "I feel like I been rode hard and put away wet." I couldn't fully translate this. I was from the suburbs—I had no idea whether you're supposed to dry off a horse before you put it away somewhere. But if Renée was trying to make herself unforgettable, she was doing it right.

Renée and I spent a lot of time that fall driving in her Chrysler, the kind of mile-wide ride southern daddies like their girls to drive around in. She would look out the window and say, "It's sunny, let's go driving"—and then we'd actually do it. She loved to hit the highway and would say things like, "Let's open 'er up." Or we would just drive around aimlessly in the Blue Ridge mountains. She loved to take sharp corners, something her grandpa had taught her back in West Virginia. He could steer with just one index finger on the wheel. I would start to feel a little dizzy as the roads started to twist at funny angles, but Renée would just accelerate and cackle, "We're shittin' in tall cotton now!"

We would always sing along to the radio. I was eager to be

her full-time Pip, but I had a lot to learn about harmony. Whenever we tried "California Dreamin'," I could never remember
whether I was the Mamas or the Papas. I had never sung duets
before. She did her best to whip me into shape.

"They could never be!"

"What she was!"

"Was!"

"Was!"

"To!"

"To!"

"To!"

"No, *no*, damn it! I'm Oates!"

"I thought *I* was Oates."

"You started as Hall. You have to stay Hall."

We never resolved that dispute. We both always wanted to be
Oates. Believe me, you don't want to hear the fights we had over
England Dan and John Ford Coley.

Have you ever been in a car with a southern girl blasting
through South Carolina when Lynyrd Skynyrd's "Call Me the
Breeze" comes on the radio? Sunday afternoon, sun out, windows down, nowhere to hurry back to? I never had. I was
twenty-three. Renée turned up the radio and began screaming
along. Renée was driving. She always preferred driving, since
she said I drove like an old Irish lady. I thought to myself, Well, I
have wasted my whole life up to this moment. Any other car I've
ever been in was just to get me here, any road I've ever been on

was just to get me here, any other passenger seat I've ever sat on, I was just riding here. I barely recognized this girl sitting next to me, screaming along to the piano solo.

I thought, There is nowhere else in the universe I would rather be at this moment. I could count the places I would not rather be. I've always wanted to see New Zealand, but I'd rather be here. The majestic ruins of Machu Picchu? I'd rather be here. A hillside in Cuenca, Spain, sipping coffee and watching leaves fall? Not even close. There is nowhere else I could imagine wanting to be besides here in this car, with this girl, on this road, listening to this song. If she breaks my heart, no matter what hell she puts me through, I can say it was worth it, just because of right now. Out the window is a blur and all I can really hear is this girl's hair flapping in the wind, and maybe if we drive fast enough the universe will lose track of us and forget to stick us somewhere else.

personics

A SIDE ONE DATE/TIME	**B** SIDE TWO DATE/TIME
Beach Boys: "Don't Worry Baby"	• Holy Modal Rounders: "Bird Song"
Stray Cats: "I Won't Stand in Your Way"	• Tom Waits: "The Piano Has Been
Isaac Hayes: "Don't Let Go"	• Drinking"
The Undisputed Truth: "Smiling Faces	• Ten City: "Right Back to You"
Sometimes"	• Aretha Franklin: "Angel"
The Isley Brothers: "This Old Heart of	•
Mine (Is Weak for You)"	•
Honey Cone: "Want Ads"	•
Lyle Lovett: "God Will"	•
The Barbarians: "Moulty"	•
	•
	•

▌ *brought this Personics tape* home to Renée as a present from Boston. The Personics fad didn't last long, but everybody got one that summer. You went to the record store, flipped through the catalog of available songs, some costing $1.75, some $1.15, some just 75 cents. You filled out your order form, handed it to the clerk, and a few hot minutes later you had your own Personics Custom Cassette with a foxy silver-and-turquoise label. *Toast in the Machine*, my tape from the Tower Records on Newbury Street, is labeled: "Made by the Personics System Especially for: RENÉE." Très romantique!

Personics seemed incredibly high-tech at the time, but really, it was just another temporary technological mutation designed to do the same thing music always does, which is allow emotionally warped people to communicate by bombarding each other with pitiful cultural artifacts that in a saner world would be forgotten before they even happened. The worst song on this tape is "Bird Song" by the Holy Modal Rounders, which I had never even heard before; I included it because I was curious how bad a song had to be to cost only 50 cents in the Personics booklet. It's two minutes and thirty-eight seconds of giggly hippie folk shit; I think it had a whistling solo, but I don't have the stomach to listen again to find out. I guess you had to be there, and by "there" I mean "dangerously baked for about three months in 1969." This tape doesn't exactly flow; it's just a bunch of burnt offerings to this goddess girl.

I realize it's frowned on to choose a mate based on something superficial like the music they love. But superficiality has been good to me. In the animal kingdom, Renée and I would have recognized each other's scents; for us, it was a matter of having the same favorite Meat Puppets album. Music was a physical bond between us, and the fact that she still owned her childhood 45 of Andy Gibb's "I Just Want to Be Your Everything" was tantamount to an arranged marriage. The idea that we might not belong together never really crossed my mind.

—

I went home with Renée, and she drove me around her home-town, three hours southwest of Charlottesville, down in the New River Valley. We drove around Pulaski County. We went to dinner at the Pizza Den and ate fried potato wedges at Wade's. Gary Clark, who played for the Washington Redskins, was from Pulaski County, and his mom had a sporting goods store right next to Wade's, so we checked it out. The closer we got to Pulaski County, the sharper Renée's accent got. She started using words like "reckon." I even heard her say "dad gum it" once, in the Safe-way parking lot. We stopped at gas stations along the way and she'd buy Hank Williams or Dwight Yoakam tapes to play until we got near enough to a town to pick up some radio.

Her people were from Greenbrier County, West Virginia, hardcore Appalachian coal country, where her grandfathers were miners. Her parents, Buddy and Nadine Crist, went to work in Washington, D.C., out of high school, and met in the Depart-ment of Commerce cafeteria. They got married at Hines Baptist Church, back in Greenbrier County, when they were both nine-teen and just before Buddy was transferred to Georgia. Her high school boyfriends were all football players. Her kind of guy drove a truck and wore thermals; she was always amused when she saw thermals in the J. Crew catalog, tastefully renamed "waffle weave." Every September, no matter who her boyfriend was, the same thing would happen—he'd be out sick from school the first day of buck season, along with all the other guys.

Renée considered herself open-minded to be dating a dude who had never shot anything.

When Renée drove me out to Pulaski County to meet her folks, she warned me that her dad was a boyfriend killer. She was right. He looked like Jim Rockford. At our first meeting he shook my hand and went right back into the story he was telling, about one of his least favorite relatives, Uncle Amos, a professional dynamiter whose South Carolina vanity plate read I BLAST. Buddy snorted, "He's shithead number two." I came to play ball, so I got right in there and asked, "Who's shithead number one?"

Buddy nodded in Renée's direction. "Her last boyfriend."

I swallowed my face into the back of my throat. That night, I slept in Nadine's sewing room. Monday morning, Renée got the lowdown from her mom. All Buddy had said about me was, "Well, better than the last one."

We went to a couple of family reunions that summer. We rolled out to West Virginia, and she took me to the famous gas station in Hughart country where the locals say Hank Williams stopped for gas on New Year's Eve 1953, in the middle of his fatal all-night ride in that long black limousine. Renée's family reunions were fun because they were all about music. Her dad would bring his guitar, and so would all her uncles—Dalton, Zennis, Troy, Kermit, and Grover—and her Aunt Caroline. By day, they stood in a circle and sang "Sweet Thing," with cousin Jerry taking the Ernest Tubb part and Aunt Caroline taking the Loretta Lynn part. At night, we stayed up late in somebody's motel room and they sang the old songs they grew up singing together, trying to remember their old harmony parts, and taught one another new radio songs. Uncle Grover's lead vocal was "Cool Water," by Sons of the Pioneers. Everybody sang on "Rocky Top." Renée's dad played a few songs, including a sad song about the coal mines he'd written for his father and one called "Itty Bitty Girl" that he wrote for Renée when she was a baby. He did one of his favorites, the old Waylon Jennings–Willie Nelson tune "Good Hearted Woman," and busted out a Porter Wagoner song I'd never heard, "The Cold Hard Facts of Life," which rhymes with "knife," which is what you get offed with when you mess with another man's "wife." I assumed Buddy meant it as a warning. He also dedicated a song to me, a rowdy version of "Red Necks, White Socks and Blue Ribbon Beer."

After she told her grandmother I was an Irish Catholic boy, her grandmother said, "You know, the Catholics killed the Christians in Spain." I had no idea what she meant, but fortunately, she didn't seem to hold me personally responsible.

Renée didn't just sit back and wait for adventures to happen. She covered ground and took me with her. Renée drove me out to Danville to find a reclusive old fifties rockabilly singer she worshipped, Janis Martin. Janis invited us in for coffee and told us stories about Patsy Cline and Ruth Brown and Elvis Elvis Elvis while her prize greyhounds bit my ankles.

Janis Martin nodded in my direction and told Renée, "He
don't say much, do he? But he's got a sweet smile. I think he
likes me."

Renée nodded and smiled. "Oh, he likes you."

Janis said, "He's thinking, hell, she's old but she's fine. The
tits ain't bad."

Renée said, "Definitely the tits."

We visited each other's rivers, the New River and An Beithe.
Water was important to our ancestors. Renée's people worried
about droughts, mine worried about floods. Some places you
don't miss your water till the well runs dry, but in the old country, my people lived in fear of water. You had to build your house
close enough to water so you could go fetch some, but on a hill
big enough so you wouldn't get flooded. It was a guessing
game—estimate too low and you lose your whole family. That's
why Auntie Peggy, still living in the old boireen in Kealduve
Upper, refused to allow indoor plumbing right up to her dying
day, which was in 1987. Whenever anybody suggested indoor
plumbing, she always said, "Sure we'll be drowned in our
beds!"

That's the way they did it in the old country. Two people
battle the elements that are trying to kill them, and if one of
them weakens, the other dies. If they stay strong, they get to die
some other way. That was romance. My grandparents stayed in
love for over sixty years.

a little down,
a little duvet

A SIDE ONE DATE/TIME	B SIDE TWO DATE/TIME
Chris Bell: "You and Your Sister"	• Big Star: "I'm In Love with a Gurl"
Yo La Tengo: "Satellite"	• The dB's: "From a Window to a Screen"
Big Star: "Nighttime"	• Billie Holiday: "These Foolish Things"
Aerosmith: "Angel"	• Roxy Music: "More Than This"
The Beatles: "Tell Me What You See"	• Matthew Sweet: "Your Sweet Voice"
Style Council: "You're the Best Thing"	• George Jones: "Color of the Blues"
Meat Puppets: "This Day"	• Yo La Tengo: "Did I Tell You"
R.E.M.: "Talk About the Passion"	• Ray Charles: "Carryin' the Load"
Otis Redding: "Come to Me"	• Prince: "Slow Love"
Yo La Tengo: "The Summer"	• Big Star: "Blue Moon"
Al Green: "You Ought to Be with Me"	• Marshall Crenshaw: "All I Know
Van Morrison: "Sweet Thing"	• Right Now"
Matthew Sweet: "Winona"	• The Beatles: "All My Loving"
Bonnie Raitt: "I Can't Make You	• Al Green: "Let's Stay Together"
Love Me"	• Dusty Springfield: "So Much Love"
	• Red Hot Chili Peppers: "Under the
	• Bridge"
	• Yo La Tengo: "Yellow Sarong"
	• Big Star: "Thirteen"

Renée made this tape for us to listen to while falling asleep, and it served us well on many nights. It's a tape full of soothing soul and vintage country and whispery rock and private jokes and intimate history. Some of the choices I didn't like at the time, such as Aerosmith's "Angel," but they all flow together in my memory now. I think about this tape years later, when I'm interviewing Aerosmith, and they tell me how much they hate "Angel." Steven Tyler tells me, "Sometimes a heavy leather biker guy with tattoos will come up to me and say, 'Oh, man, let me tell you my favorite song,' and every time, I know it's gonna be 'Angel.' And I just gulp, and I don't know what to say. Ugh, *that* one?"

I wonder whether I should tell Steven Tyler I used to hate "Angel," too, but after my wife put it on this romantic mix tape, tucked in between Big Star and the Beatles, I fell in love with it. I decide not to tell him. I'm sure somewhere in his cosmic rock-star heart, he knows the whole story.

"Thirteen" was the song we chose as the first dance at our wedding.

I never planned to get married when I was only twenty-five, and I'm not sure exactly how it happened—neither of us ever officially proposed, or anything dramatic like that. It started off as a playful fantasy we talked about. Then the fantasy became a plan, the way fantasies sometimes do, and the plan became a future. It didn't hit us as the climax of anything, just the celebration of something that had already happened to us. I guess we hoped the celebration would help us understand what had happened.

It really started one Saturday when we were driving around

in the mountains off Route 33, listening to a Marshall Crenshaw song called "Lesson Number One." It's a sad rockabilly ballad about how lying is bad, and telling the truth is lesson number one. We started talking about the song, and I carelessly said, "I've never lied to you."

"Yeah?" she said. "And you never will?"

"No, I never will."

Then we were both quiet for a few minutes. I was afraid that I'd just ruined everything; it was the first time either of us had ever promised anything. But it felt all right. I guess making little promises made us braver about the bigger ones.

There was never any epiphanic moment when we decided we should get married, no bolt of lightning. As soon as we started talking about it, we started trying to talk ourselves out of it, but we failed. Irish people marry late, as a rule. We have that potato-famine DNA from the old country, that mentality where you don't give birth to anything until you have the potatoes all stored up to feed it. My ancestors were all shepherds who got married in their thirties and then stayed together for life, who had long and happy marriages, no doubt because they were already deaf. My grandparents courted for nine years before they married in 1933. My cousin Sis Boyle in Southie was engaged for seventeen years before she finally threw caution to the wind and got hitched—and then she gave birth nine months later to the day. Renée was not psyched to hear stories like this. She informed me that Appalachians wed early, give birth immediately, and worry about feeding all their offspring later. Her parents met at eighteen, married at nineteen, and became parents at twenty. This terrified me. Between the two of us, we had three master's degrees, thousands of records, and no future.

I kept thinking of an old Robert Mitchum cowboy movie where he goes back to see the farmhouse where he was born and finds the house falling apart and an old man living in it by himself. "Lonely place," Robert Mitchum says. The old man says, "Nothing wrong with a lonely place as long as it's private. That's why I never married. Marriage is lonely, but it ain't private." That was always my most intense fear about getting married: When everything sucked and I was by myself, I thought, Well, at least I don't have another miserable person to worry about. I figured if you give up your private place and it still turns out to be lonely, you're just screwed. So I felt safer not even thinking about it. No doubt about it, the idea of staying together was scary. But we also didn't want to wait around for a few years to see if it was going to happen. Why not just *make* it happen? It felt disingenuous to keep saying, "If we're still together next year . . ." since we knew we *wanted* to be together next year. Pretending to keep those options open became dead weight.

We were just a couple of fallen angels, rolling the dice of our lives. We'd heard all the horror stories of early marriages and fast divorces and broken hearts. But we knew none of them would happen to us, because as Dexy's Midnight Runners sang to Eileen, we were far too young and clever. What if we just decide *not* to fall apart? What if we decide *not* to wait to see what happens, but instead decide what we want to happen and then decide how to make it happen? Like Burt Reynolds says to Jerry Reed in *Smokey and the Bandit*, "We ain't never not made it before, have we?"

So I gave Renée my grandmother's ring. My grandfather was crazy about Renée, at least partly because she was practically a foot shorter than all his granddaughters, so he could lean over and talk right into her ear. I knew my grandmother would have loved Renée, but I still hoped I wasn't letting her down. Renée and I were acting like a couple of foolhardy American brats. Nana had always warned me: Never marry an American girl. "These American girls are lazy!" she would fume. "They won't cook or clean. You need an Irish girl."

When Renée and I talked about it years later, we agreed on one point: We were insane. Renée always said, "If any of our kids want to get married when they're twenty-five, we'll have to lock them in the attic." We were just kids, and everybody who came to the wedding was guilty of shameful if not criminal negligence—look at the shiny pretty toaster, isn't it cute to see the babies playing with it in the bathtub? Jesus, people! There is such a thing as "tough love." But for whatever reason, nobody tried to stop us, or even talk sense into us. Instead, everybody wanted to help us out. We had no money, so all our friends did wedding favors for us. Our friend Gavin offered to DJ the wedding. Neither of us wanted to go crazy planning a wedding—we had our hands full planning the marriage.

I tried to talk Renée into doing our wedding dance to Van Halen's "Everybody Wants Some" because I had a romantic vision of us wangoing our fandango to the part where Alex Van Halen is playing the bongos and David Lee Roth is doing his heartfelt "I like the way the line runs up the back of the stock-ing" monologue. But Renée quickly squashed that idea—no romance in the girl. So Big Star's "Thirteen" it was, the song that brought us together. We rented the university chapel for an hour, which cost a hundred bucks, and booked a reception at the Best Western down the street. For the ceremony Renée chose a Baptist hymn I'd never heard of, "Shall We Gather at the River," and we had fun picking out readings from Wallace Stevens and Virginia Woolf. We were looking forward to drawing up a prenuptial agreement, but unfortunately, we found out you can't get one unless you actually own something. Renée picked out a tux for me—I hadn't worn one since the Walpole High senior prom (theme: "We've Got Tonight")—and she selected a morn-ing coat because it made me look like Janet Jackson in her "Escapade" video.

All I remember about the actual wedding is standing there on the altar steps like Enzo the baker in *The Godfather* stood on the hospital stairs with Al Pacino, waiting for the Turk's hit men to come, trying to scare the hit men away by looking like they were ready for them. We both felt like Enzo that day. He's a baker; he doesn't know anything about guns. He just came to bring some flowers for his Don, who did him a big favor on Connie's wedding day. Now he and Pacino are standing on the stairs, shaking, pretending they know what they're doing. They don't fool each other, but maybe they can fool everybody else.

———

During the wedding Renée put my ring on my right hand. She started whispering, "Wrong hand! Wrong hand!" I whispered back, "Let's switch it *later*," but she insisted on grabbing my hand, slipping the ring off, and putting it on my left hand, all in the middle of the ceremony. Nobody in the crowd noticed this. You did good, Enzo.

When we got to the Best Western, we hit the dance floor, as Gavin favored us with our special request, James Brown's "I'm a Greedy Man." The Godfather of Soul laid out his three-point program for domestic bliss:

- Don't leave the homework undone,
- Don't tell the neighbors,

and, most crucially,

- You got to have something to sit on before
  I carry you home.

Everybody shook it to the Go-Go's and the Human League and Chuck Berry, and we drank champagne and Gavin played Al Green's version of "I Want to Hold Your Hand" at least four times. I danced with Renée's mom to the Chuck Berry song "Nadine." My sisters told me I needed to make a speech to the guests. I began by quoting the rapper Kool Moe Dee; my sisters told me that was a nice speech and cut me off. Gavin put on

C&C Music Factory's "Everybody Dance Now" and my Uncle Ray took that as a cue to start the electric slide. (Uncle Ray and the electric slide go together like a 1976 Ford Pinto and a box of matches.) At any wedding we attend, my family is the problem table, the one everybody gradually drifts away from out of self-preservation. It's a proud family tradition. Now this was *our* wedding, and nobody could stop us. Giving us a crate of champagne and a dance floor was like handing a madman the keys to a 747 and saying, "Now, seriously, dude, don't crash it. Promise?"

Right before the party broke up, Renée's Uncle Troy came up and gave her a big hug and whispered into her ear. I was touched. I didn't realize he was saying, "Go easy on the boy."

After the reception our friends drove us to the Eastern Standard, the bar where we met. The bartender on duty was Ruby, one of our favorites, a profane and excellent old lady who didn't give a damn about our precious memories. Ruby, She-Wolf of the SS. Ruby put the "freak" in "frequently drunk and belligerent." Since Virginia state law prohibits a bartender from consuming alcohol behind the bar, she instead lit up a big fatty and ignored all our drunken requests to play the Big Star tape. There was a big party across the street that night, at Silver Fox, the only drag joint in town, and since the club didn't have a liquor license the room was full of Chers and Jackies popping over to the Eastern Standard for a drink. Cornered on separate sides of the room, Renée and I watched our friends mingle, and occasionally locked eyes, trying to spot which guests were in the running for wedding nookie. Renée quizzed the Jews about what "mazel tov" means, the Baptists quizzed me about whether Renée was now obligated to bear Catholic babies and donate them to the Vatican, and the southerners quizzed the northerners about why nobody really eats grits. Around eleven, everybody drained their glasses and went off to the mall to see *Terminator 2*.

Renée and I stayed behind for one more bourbon and ginger, which neither of us had any appetite to finish. We had waited all day to get just one minute to ourselves, but neither of us could think of a thing to say.

"Why did he kiss the book?" Renée finally asked me.

"Excuse me?"

"Father Cunningham, he kissed the book."

"It's a standard thing."

"Does it mean I'm Catholic now? Because if he made me Catholic without asking, my mama is gonna be pissed."

"He made you a bishop."

Renée poked her ice cubes with a plastic pirate sword and put her head on my shoulder. She asked me, "Was Mel gay?"

"You have a question, Your Holiness?"

"Mel. From Mel's diner. Kiss my grits."

"You mean Vic Tayback."

"No, just Mel."

"I don't think so."

"Mel never got any chicks. EVER."

"He was a hardworking man. Devoted to his diner."

"He never got any chicks. He never hung around anybody except Alice, with her show tunes. And Vera, with the tap dancing."

"He had Flo."

"Flo was a total drag queen."

"I just don't see it."

"Queer as a three-dollar bill, honey," Ruby said. "Last call."

Nobody remembered to give us a lift home. The last bus had stopped running hours ago. So I grabbed Renée's hand, or maybe she grabbed mine, and we walked. Maybe it took an hour or two; neither of us was wearing a watch, so I don't know. We were too tired to gossip, so we sang songs we knew, like "O.P.P." and "I Just Want to Be Your Everything." Turned out we both remembered the words to a bunch of other Andy Gibb songs.

If I had my way, the story would end here. Renée was always braver. She always wanted to know what happens next.

that's entertainment

A SIDE ONE DATE/TIME	**B** SIDE TWO DATE/TIME
Morrissey: "That's Entertainment"	• Teenage Fanclub: "Everybody's Fool,"
Unrest: "Yes She Is My Skinhead Girl," •	"God Knows It's True"
"Sex Machine"	• The Perfect Disaster: "Takin' Over"
The Dead C.: "Scarey New," "Phantom	• Yo La Tengo: "Yellow Sarong," "The
Power"	• Summer," "Oklahoma, USA,"
Love Child: "Know It's Alright"	• "Ecstasy Blues"
Pavement: "Angel Carver Blues/Mellow	• Superchunk: "Slack Motherfucker"
Jazz Docent"	• Urge Overkill: "The Candidate"
Sonic Youth: "Personality Crisis"	• Blake Babies: "I'm Not Your Mother,"
Nirvana: "Sliver"	• "I'll Take Anything," "Gimme Some
Teenage Fanclub: "Everything Flows"	• Mirth"
Pavement: "Debris Slide"	• The Pooh Sticks: "Young People," "The
Superchunk: "Cool"	• Rhythm Of Love"
Unrest: "Cherry Cherry"	•
Royal Trux: "Lick My Boots"	•

Now that we were married, Renée stopped having dreams about her ex-boyfriends every night. She was pissed about that. So was I. The months leading up to the wedding had been a pageant of highly entertaining (for me) and traumatic (for her) dreams, which she confessed with shame every morning. They all had the same plot: Renée trysts with a boy from her past, he begs her to run away with him, she thinks about it, and then she decides instead to move on to her future with me. She thought these dreams were guilty secrets. I thought they were funny. I loved meeting these clowns. My favorite was the volleyball player from Roanoke. The last time she booty-called him, he said he was busy—he didn't want to miss the farewell episode of *Magnum, P.I.* Years after the fact, Renée was still fuming. I wanted to shake his hand. This was my competition? No wonder I got a shot. Compared to her memories, I felt like Pelé kicking a couple around with the 1981 Tampa Bay Rowdies.

Now we were married, and the dreams stopped. I guess she'd said her goodbyes. We both missed these boys. Now we were alone with each other.

Which meant we had all these neighbors to deal with. The old lady next door dropped by with a plate of muffins one Sunday afternoon, right in the middle of *Studs.* Renée explained that in the South, this is normal—you just drop in on your married neighbors. I was aghast. I was a husband in the South now. We had married into this alien landscape with its strange customs. Had I chosen this? Had Renée? It felt like a hangover from a country song: You pass out on the train, miss your stop, wake up in a town you've never heard of, and that's where you live now. Renée and I *were* just passing through, on our way somewhere, but suddenly we *lived* here.

As newlyweds, we crammed into Renée's basement on High-land Avenue. It was the first place we ever had to ourselves, with side two of Earth, Wind & Fire's *Greatest Hits, Volume 1* on the stereo, never needing to be flipped—we just lifted the needle every eighteen minutes. Renée had a pantyhose job as a parale-gal at a law firm. At work, she turned the radio down low so she could listen to my radio show, and I serenaded her with long-distance dedications like Frightwig's "My Crotch Does Not Say Go." Around five, I drove downtown to pick her up from work, and then we could go anywhere we wanted. It was too hot to go home until the sun went down, so we usually hit the Fashion Square Mall, where we'd sit on a bench, basking in the free air-conditioning, breathing in the scent of cookie-corns and cinna-clusters and crunch-o-cottons, chattering to keep our minds from wandering places we couldn't afford to go. For pinball, we hit the Seminole Theater, where we could play the *Rollerball* machine all night without buying a movie ticket. If we were feel-ing lazy, we just went to MJ Design to browse through all the leopardskin fun fur.

Our backyard looked into the woods, and we'd sit out there when it got too humid to breathe inside. Charlottesville turns into a rain forest every summer; the sea winds blow in from Tidewater, a few hundred miles to the east, and then they run slam into the Blue Ridge, so all the hot, wet air just hovers over Charlottesville. We'd look out across our neighbors' yards and try to imagine their lives. Did they really *live* here, call it home?

Or were they on their way to bigger things, like us? Did they get stuck here on their way somewhere else, or was this the town where they arrived and said, This is the place? Did they give up and blame each other? Were they lying low and planning their next move?

I was still serfing away at grad school. My friends and I assumed that we would soon be tenured professors, which is an excellent life goal—it's like planning to be Cher. You think, I'm going to wear beads and fringed gowns, and sing "Gypsies, Tramps, and Thieves" on the way to work every morning, and then one day, I'm going to get a call saying, "Congratulations! You're Cher! Can you make it to Vegas by showtime?"

Renée and I would shiver in the air-conditioning of the Fashion Square Mall and talk about how excellent it was going to be when we finally got out of Charlottesville. We'd go to the early bird special at the Chicken House, over in the Sears end of the mall. It was cheap, and we liked being surrounded by crotchety old couples. Someday, we'd be one of them. Meanwhile, we couldn't believe how exciting it was to be together, a pair of young Americruisers on a roll. We'd lived for just twenty-five years; we weren't planning to die for fifty more. We danced and drank and went to rock shows. Our lives were just beginning, our favorite moment was right now, our favorite songs were unwritten.

That summer we got our dog, and our new favorite band.

"I want to meet our dog," Renée said one night. We were sitting in the Fashion Square Mall parking lot, around midnight, the windows rolled down.

"We don't have a dog," I said.

"That's why I want to meet him."

"I hate dogs."

"You're gonna love dogs."

"I grew up with dogs."

"Yappy little northern things. Wait till you meet Duane."

Duane Allman, the guitarist for the Allman Brothers, the sweet blond Georgia angel who played the solos on "Whipping Post" and "You Don't Love Me" and "Blue Sky." We drove to the SPCA and went looking for Duane.

"I hate dogs."

"This dog is gonna be Duane Allman. A southern dog. He's gonna sleep in the sun all day. He's gonna be a ramblin' man."

"Duane Allman didn't play on 'Ramblin' Man,' actually. That was Dickey Betts."

"You're such a boy."

Duane Allman was a beagle. The ladies at the SPCA put her on a leash and had Renée take her out for a walk around the grounds. Her name used to be "Dutchess," with a T. She was about a year old and tall for a beagle, and she wagged her tail as soon as she saw Renée. We walked a couple of dogs that day, but none of them had fit the name. This one was Duane.

"The next dog will be Ronnie Van Zandt," Renée said on the way home while Duane was in the backseat getting carsick.

My interest in dogs defined the term "scant." Interests don't come any scanter. I was hoping Duane Allman would change my mind. She didn't. Duane was nowhere near mellow—she was a high-strung little bundle of nightmares in fur. She was not so much Duane Allman; more like Teenage Jesus and the Jerks. Duane bit the cable guy and banged her head against the screen door; Renée didn't notice. Dog love is blind. For that matter, dog love is stupid. Duane and I never would have tolerated each other if we'd had a choice. But what could we do? We were two animals in love with the same girl.

Now there were three of us, and the apartment was even smaller, so we turned up the stereo and made it a little louder. Like all our friends in Charlottesville, we lived for music. In the summer of 1991, the world was teeming with hot young guitar bands. We didn't know "Smells Like Teen Spirit" was on the way in a few months. We just knew that after a few years of rock bands sounding smug and doddering, there was something new in the air. We played Nirvana's "Sliver" single a lot. They did not sound like a band that was getting ready to challenge the world. Truth be told, they sounded kind of like the Lemonheads. But that was fine. This was the music we'd fallen in love to, the music that brought us together, and now there was more of it around than ever.

We waited all that summer for the Pavement show. The flier was up all over town:

We mean it man

PAVEMENT

with very special guests

ROYAL TRUX

THURSDAY, AUGUST 29

$5, only $4 for anyone wearing a WTJU T-shirt

**Basically he's a nice suburban kid
who got hold of a guitar and some heroin
and went a little bit wrong.**

The night of the show, the floor was abuzz with anticipation. None of us in the crowd knew what Pavement looked like, or even who was in the band. They put out mysterious seven-inch singles without any band info or photos, just credits for instruments like "guitar slug," "psued-piano gritt-gitt," "keybored," "chime scheme," and "last crash simbiosis." We assumed that they were manly and jaded, that they would stare at the floor and make abstract boy noise. That would be a good night out.

Royal Trux went on a few hours late, which I'm sure had nothing to do with buying drugs in Richmond. They were great, like a scuzz-rock Katrina and the Waves. The peroxide girl in the football jersey jumped around and screamed while the boy with the scary home-cut bangs played his guitar and tried to stay out of her way. She threw a cymbal at him. We wanted to take them home for a bath, a hot meal, and a blood change.

But Pavement was nothing at all like we pictured them. They were a bunch of foxy dudes, and they were *into it*. As soon as they hit the stage, you could hear all the girls in the crowd ovulate in unison. There were five or six of them up there, some banging on guitars, some just clapping their hands or singing along. They did not stare at the floor. They were there to make some noise and have some fun. They had fuzz and feedback and unironically beautiful sha-la-la melodies. The bassist looked just like Renée's high school boyfriend. Stephen Malkmus leaned into the mike, furrowed his brows, and sang lyrics like "I only really want you for your rock and roll" or "When I fuck you once it's never enough / When I fuck you two times it's always too much." The songs were all either fast or sad, because all songs should be either fast or sad. Some of the fast ones were sad, too.

Afterward, we staggered to the parking lot in total silence. When we got to the car, Renée spoke up in a mournful voice: "I don't think The Feelies are ever gonna be good enough again."

Our friend Joe in New York sent us a tape, a third-generation dub of the Pavement album *Slanted and Enchanted*. Renée and I decided this was our favorite tape of all time. The guitars were all boyish ache and shiver. The vocals were funny bad poetry sung through a Burger World drive-through mike. The melodies were full of surfer-boy serenity, dreaming through a haze of tape hiss and mysterious amp noise. This was the greatest band ever, obviously. And they didn't live twenty years ago, or ten years ago, or five years ago. They were right now. They were ours.

I think about those days, and I think about a motto etched onto the sleeve of one of those Pavement singles: I AM MADE OF BLUE SKY AND HARD ROCK AND I WILL LIVE THIS WAY FOREVER.

the comfort zone

A SIDE ONE DATE/TIME	**B** SIDE TWO DATE/TIME
Vanessa Williams: "The Comfort Zone"	• Tom Cochrane: "Life Is a Highway"
	• Escape Club: "I'll Be There"
The KLF featuring Tammy Wynette: "Justified and Ancient"	• TLC: "Baby Baby Baby"
	• En Vogue: "Giving Him Something He Can Feel"
U2: "One"	
Hi-Five: "I Can't Wait Another Minute"	• Lionel Richie: "Do It to Me"
	• A.L.T.: "Tequila"
Kris Kross: "Jump"	• George Michael and Elton John: "Don't Let the Sun Go Down on Me"
Enigma: "Sadeness Part 1"	•
Paula Abdul: "The Promise of a New Day"	•
	• Trey Lorenz: "Someone to Hold"
Linear: "TLC"	• Corina: "Temptation"
Fine Young Cannibals: "She Drives Me Crazy"	• Nikki: "Notice Me"
	• Natural Selection: "Do Anything"
Mariah Carey: "Love Takes Time"	• Mint Condition: "Breakin' My Heart (Pretty Brown Eyes)"
Siouxsie and the Banshees: "Kiss Them for Me"	• Hi-Five: "I Like The Way (The Kissing Game)"
Prince: "Cream"	•
Madonna: "This Used to Be My Playground"	•
	•
Right Said Fred: "I'm Too Sexy"	•
Sir Mix-A-Lot: "Baby Got Back"	•

The Comfort Zone was a dishes tape, maybe the finest of all dishes tapes, guaranteed to get me up to my elbows in Dawn Power Sudsing Formula and through the loading of the drying rack. I cranked it on the boombox we kept on the kitchen counter, right next to the sink. I taped most of it from Casey Kasem's *American Top 40* countdown on Z-95, our local Top 40 station, with Casey nattering between songs. But that just adds to the ambience, since for any pop devotee, Casey's voice is music of the spheres. This tape counts down the hits from coast to coast! As the numbers get smaller, the hits get bigger! And we don't stop! Till we reach the top!

Like all radio tapes, it's a mixed bag. Disco scam artists, hair-metal schnauzers in red leather chaps, gangstas, ravers, fly-by-night pop smoothies, cartoon lip-synchers, sequin divas, flukes, hacks, one-hit scandals—we loved it all. Nobody remembers The KLF today, but they made one of the decade's most sublime one-shots in 1992 with their hit "Justified and Ancient." A couple of British art-school poseurs hire Tammy Wynette to sing an incredibly beautiful disco song about an ice cream van? Genius! And of course, it became a gigantic international hit. Only in the nineties, brothers and sisters. Nobody ever took this music seriously, but we loved it anyway: Vanilla Williams, Paula Abominable, Kris Kross, my beloved Hi-Five.

In some circles, admitting you love Top 40 radio is tanta-mount to bragging you gave your grandmother the clap, in church, in the front row at your aunt's funeral, but those are the circles I avoid like the plague or, for that matter, the clap. The beauty of Top 40 is you don't have to be any kind of great artist to make a great record—indeed, great artistness is just a pain in the ass, which is why moron-rock choo-choo hack Tom Cochrane sounds right at home here with his idiot anthem, while U2 sound like Jesuits trying to act cool for the youth-group retreat. Tom Cochrane had nothing to say, plus a stupid way of saying it, but he helped me get the dishes done. As Casey Kasem would say, he kept my feet on the ground, and kept me reaching for the stars—even with my hands full of soap suds.

Z-95 was the only Top 40 station in town, and my wife and I loved it fiercely. Z-95 played hits like "I'm Too Sexy" and "Baby Got Back" and "Justified and Ancient" once an hour. They also constantly played this terrible British techno hit called "Groovy Train" by The Farm. Or maybe it was "Groovy Farm" by The Train—how would I know? Z-95 played all sorts of alleged hits that didn't exist in the real Billboard Top 40 charts, songs our friends in the big cities never heard of. We thought 2 In A Room's "Wiggle It" was the biggest hit in the world. It wasn't. We thought Martika's "Love . . . Thy Will Be Done" was the musical-youth anthem of the mid-to-late spring of 1992. It wasn't. We pitied the fools in New York and L.A. who had no idea Hi-Five were the world's greatest rock and roll band. MTV wouldn't touch this stuff. But what did they know? This was a golden age, and just by being stuck out in the middle of no-where, we were right in the heat of the action. Nobody remembers, nobody cares, and I guess that's fine with me. But I could hum Nikki's "Notice Me" for you. A few years ago there were two of us.

One night Renée and I were watching the En Vogue video where they shimmy in a swank club wearing those foxy red dresses. She said, "They're not wearing underwear."

"They're not? How do you know?"

"I just know."

"They're not?"

"They're not."

I looked, but I could not see. I guess a woman just knows these things. Maybe it was the way the girls grind their hips, to and fro, in a way that underwear simply cannot contain; maybe it was the absence of panty lines. Renée wouldn't tell me.

There's also a scene in the video where one of the guys in the audience slips his wedding ring off his finger and hides it in his pocket. Renée hated that scene, but I loved it because it reminded me that it was time to do the dishes. Whenever I did dishes, I had to slip off my wedding ring and put it on the microwave so it wouldn't go down the drain. So, I think this is the perfect pop song—it reminds me of not wearing underwear, and it also reminds me of the dishes. What more could you want?

I come from a long line of dish-washing men. When I was a little kid, I was amazed at the energy my grandfather had for washing dishes. My mom always told me, "He does it for the peace." I didn't understand until I was grown-up and a husband myself, when it made perfect sense. I found I had joined a club, a tribe extending backward through the centuries, mild-mannered Irish men married to loud, tempestuous Irish women. Sometimes, the only way to escape is to turn on a couple of jets of extremely loud water and disappear into the sound for a few hours. Sometimes, when Renée and I were fighting, I would wash dishes that weren't even dirty, just to create a little noise.

Renée and I were surprised at all the drama we had to deal with, just living together in our tiny room. For one thing, we always argued about the telephone. I'm not much of a phone person. I always vowed if I ever met a woman who ignored a ringing phone for me, she was the one. But of course, this never happened, and I fell for a woman who would have dropped a scalpel into my spleen in the middle of performing open-heart surgery on me to grab the phone. You know the Prince song where the girl's phone rings but she tells him, "Whoever's calling couldn't be as cute as you?" I long to live out this moment in real life. But I doubt it ever happened to Prince either. I bet even Apollonia got the phone.

Neither of us was a skilled fighter. My ancestors were neither warriors nor kings. I am descended from generations of peace-loving shepherds who tended their flocks in the hills of Keal-duve and never killed anybody. Their strength was in their patience. Growing up I never got into fights because I never

wanted to disgrace my ancestors—God knows they knew how
to disgrace themselves, and fair play to them. But they lived in
the grassy fields, so when the house was full of ugly emotions
they could step outside, smoke a pipe, kick a sheep or something, and let the air clear. Renée and I did not have a farm, or
even walls in our apartment, so we had to do our fighting in the
same room where we had to sleep and eat, and that's no good.
Her temper was a zero-to-sixty machine. We were pretty good at
keeping the two-minute fights from escalating into three-
minute fights. The problem was keeping the three-minute
fights from turning into eight-hour fights. When the air in the
house got toxic, I would go out into the driveway and sit in the
car and read, waiting for the smoke to clear.

One Saturday afternoon, I got tired of the driveway, so I said,
Fuck this, and drove to the parking lot at the Barracks Road
Shopping Center, got a cup of coffee, and locked myself in with
a book. I sat there all day, reading Shelley's *The Witch of Atlas*,
hoping for the bad blood in my head to simmer down. When the
sun went down, I still wasn't ready to go home, so I cracked the
door to turn on the inside light for as long as I could stand
the cold. After that, I turned on the engine and sat there with
it running and tried to keep reading. I turned on the radio and
heard an old 1970s hit I have loathed since my childhood:
"Hitchin' a Ride" by Vanity Fare. I hate this song. The singer
chirps about how he's stuck on the side of the road, hitchin' a
ride, since his girl threw him out. "Ride, ride, ride. Hitchin' a ride."

There's a flute solo. I sat there huddling in the cold, breathing out steam, fuming, I hate this song. Then I drove home. A couple of nights later, Renée asked, "Where did you take the car the other day?" I told her. She laughed at me.

Stupid shit we used to fight about:

The Telephone: Would she stop to answer the phone in the middle of a fight about the phone? Yes, she would. This definitely proved one of us right, but I'm not sure which one.

Money: One of us was a scrimp-and-saver, the other was a big spender. Neither of us was what is known as an "earner."

Reproduction: We were programmed very differently about this one, in terms of our ancestry and culture. She was into the idea of having babies fast; I wasn't. Three or four times a year we would have a conversation about this, which would usually begin as a whimsical anecdote about a college friend's baby or a pregnant relative, and suddenly turn into the last twenty minutes of *The Wild Bunch*. Why didn't we discuss this *before* we got married? I don't know. We just didn't. Renée had this excellent country-girl pal at her mall job named Tiffany, who quit to have a baby and go on welfare. When she brought her baby to the mall to show everybody, Tiffany asked Renée how come she didn't have a baby yet. Renée said something about saving up. Tiffany said, "Aw, hon, the money always comes from somewhere!" The weird part is, not only did we both love this story, we each felt it proved us right. Strange! But true!

The Word "Repulse": I *hate* this word. I believe "repel" is a perfectly good word, and "repulsion" is the noun, as well as the title of an excellent Dinosaur Jr. song. A compulsion compels you; an impulse impels you. Nobody ever says "compulse" or "impulse" as a verb. So why would you ever say "repulse"? This word haunts me in my sleep, like a silver dagger dancing before my eyes. Renée looked it up and I was wrong. But I still kind of think I'm right.

The Word "Utilize": Even worse.

Figure Skating: She won this one. I'm glad she did. Figure skating saved us. No matter how bad a mood Renée was in, those twirls and axels melted her butter. Figure skaters were always on TV somewhere. Ice dancers were the best: brooding Slav castrati dudes with tree-trunk thighs, packed into a glittery fistful of L'Eggs, twirling feminine whisks named Natasha or Alexandra, enacting the legend of Orpheus and Eurydice to the orchestral strains of "Loving on Borrowed Time: Love Theme from *Cobra*." How did married people stay together before this shit was invented? I honestly have no idea. Renée drooled over Paul Wiley (the clean-cut American), Victor Petrenko (the ruthless Russian), Kurt Browning (the burly Canadian), and good old Scott Hamilton. That guy's enduring success as a sex symbol is the sort of thing that makes me wipe tears of joy from my eyes and proclaim, "Thumbs up, America!" For me, the ladies all dissolved into a blur of vowels and poofy skirts, except Katarina Witt. That girl had an ass on her. *The Cutting Edge* — I don't see why this isn't the most famous movie ever made. Moira Kelly as the skate princess! Brrrrrr — she's cold as ice! She's willing to sacrifice her love! D. B. Sweeney as the hockey stud! "I do two things well, babe — and skating's the other one." Can they win the medal and triple-lutz their way to love? (Of *course* they can! Pay attention!) For Renée, this flick was liquid Vicodin. We watched it several thousand times. I can still recite the whole thing from memory. "In case you can't tell . . . I'm throwing myself at you!"

TV in General: We both loved *The Banana Splits* and MTV. We disagreed about everything else. As far as I was concerned, TV had been crap ever since Freddie Prinze died. But we did our best to appreciate each other's tastes — she got me into *The Andy Griffith Show*, I got her into *Sanford and Son*. My preferred method of avoiding her shows was just to go into the kitchen and do dishes, turning the water up loud whenever Renée got hooked on a show that involved doctors, lawyers, a small town full of lovable eccentrics, or Kirstie Alley.

Getting a Dog: She won this one easily, as I've already mentioned; I thought my graceful surrender would win me a concession or two down the line. I was wrong. Renée saw the dog not as a personal victory for her, but as a huge favor she was doing me by teaching me the joys of being pissed on by an animal. This is just one of the adorable quirks of the dog, the best friend God ever gave humanity in this crazy little world. Thanks, God!

The Air-conditioning Commercial: You know this one. It comes back every spring, like the gypsy moth caterpillar. The husband and wife sit sweating at the kitchen table. She says, "Honeeeeeey, why don't we have aaaaaair-conditioning?" He says, "I'll call tomorrow." She says, "You'll call today?" He smiles and says, "I'll call today." Then he's on the phone, giving her a hearty thumbs-up, while Renée sits frozen, knuckles white on the remote, and asks, "I'm not like *her*, am I?" This question is like the cowboy in *Mulholland Drive*, who you see again one time if you do good and two times if you do bad. Answer the question wisely, and you won't have to hear it again for another year. Try to give a clever answer, and you have bigger immediate problems than the humidity index.

The Cure's "Let's Go to Bed": Similar to the above, but when she gets depressed and asks, "Honey, is this song about us?" the strategic answer is, "Yes, but so is 'Just Like Heaven.' "

Fighting: As with most couples, probably, most of our fights were not *about* anything, but rather about fighting itself. We negotiated the rules, slowly, stupidly, over time. The word "sulk" got banned early on, in the summer of 1990. "Pout" was soon to follow. "Don't start" was banned in the fall of 1992. "What is that supposed to mean?" got banned, reinstated, and banned again. "Not that again" took a few years to go on the index. "What are you thinking?" never did get banned, despite my intense lobbying efforts.

Whenever we had a fight, I could never get to sleep, so after it was over I got up, moved to the couch, fixed a sandwich, and watched TV with the sound down. One night I watched this intense Bette Davis movie, *A Stolen Life.* Even without sound, I could still follow the basic gist. There are twin Bette Davises, a good twin and an evil twin. Both are in love with Glenn Ford. They're in a boat; it's stormy; the boat capsizes. The good twin sinks under the waves and desperately reaches out her hand. The evil twin reaches down, but instead of grasping the hand, she just slides the wedding ring right off her sister's finger. Damn. That's cold-blooded, Bette Davis. Back in town, she pretends to be the good twin and gets to have post-shipwreck sex with Glenn Ford. I fell asleep, so I never found out if she got caught. After Renée died, I kept meaning to go back and watch it with the sound on, but I never did.

One night, after some fight I'd thought we'd both forgotten, Renée woke up trembling and cold. She gave me very detailed instructions about what she needed. I was to get up, go into the kitchen, open up her stash of pizza dough, and make her a pizza. This would take half an hour or so. I asked if she'd be okay by herself for that long and she promised she would call me if she couldn't make it. She was shaking. I got up and went to the kitchen.

When the pizza was done, I carried it back to bed and we ate it. Renée told me the whole time she was alone in bed, she sang a song over and over to comfort herself. She sang: "The only one who could ever reach me, was the Makin'-the-Pizza Man."

dancing with myself

AUGUST 1993

A THE SLOW AND INTROSPECTIVE BURN	B MOTIVATIONAL MADNESS
Meat Puppets: "Up on the Sun"	• Tag Team: "Whoomp! There It Is"
Penelope Houston: "Qualities of Mercy"	• Chaka Khan: "I Feel for You"
	• New York Dolls: "Trash"
The Chills: "Part Past Part Fiction"	• X: "Breathless"
Bettie Serveert: "Tom Boy"	• Jordy: "Dur Dur D'Être Bébé"
Pavement: "Box Elder"	• Snatch: "Up and Down"
Madonna: "Rain"	• RuPaul: "Supermodel"
New Order: "Regret"	• X-Ray Spex: "Oh Bondage, Up Yours!"
Juliana Hatfield: "Ugly"	• L7: "Fast and Frightening"
Lucinda Williams: "Sweet Old World"	• KC & the Sunshine Band: "Shake Your
Morrissey: "Sing Your Life"	• Booty"
Replacements: "Kiss Me on the Bus"	• Shonen Knife: "My Favorite Town
The Shams: "Time"	• Osaka"
The Smiths: "Cemetry Gates"	• Buzzcocks: "What Do I Get?"
R.E.M.: "Sitting Still"	• Blondie: "I'm Gonna Love You Too"
	• X: "In This House That I Call Home"
	• L7: "'Till the Wheels Fall Off"

O ne day we were at the Barracks Road Shopping Center when Renée called me over to the cosmetics aisle. We stared at a brightly colored plastic tube dangling from a hook. It was our first encounter with Grunge Gunk or, as it proclaimed itself on the label, "The Alternative Hair Styling Mud!" Of course we took it home ($1.75) and Renée nailed it up on the bathroom door.

It was a Grunge Gunk kind of summer.

As Lionel Richie once warned us, there comes a time when we heed a certain call. For us, that time was the summer of 1993. Our first redhead summer smelled like hair dye and nail polish. Renée had only been a redhead for a few months, but she was already burying her brunette past, and the apartment filled up with cosmetic fumes. Renée had a new job at the Fashion Square Mall, working as the Clarins girl at the Leggett makeup counter. At work, she became instant best friends with the Clinique girl, Susan, a Waynesboro muscle-car aficionado. She was fond of dispensing wisdom along the lines of: "The bullshit stops when the green light pops!" I'd go to the mall to pick up Renée, take them both a couple of coffees, and hang out while they chattered in their hot white coats. Susan would take Renée to hot-rod shows and run-what-ya-brung drag races. She brought out sides of Renée I'd never gotten to see before, and it was a sight to behold. After a night out with Susan, Renée would always come back saying things like, "If it's got tits or tires, it's gonna cost you money."

That year, the music we loved had blown up nationwide. It was a little ridiculous how formerly underground guitar rock was crashing through the boundaries. More guitar bands than ever were making noise, and more of them than ever were worth hearing. The first sign of the apocalypse had come during the

Winter Olympics when Kristi Yamaguchi, America's gold-medal ice queen, was doing her free-form routine to Edith Piaf's "Milord," and TV announcer Dick Buttons said that Kristi psyched herself up backstage by listening to her favorite band, Nirvana, on her Walkman. Renée and I just stared at each other. For her, it was an epiphanic moment—punk rock was now music that even figure-skater girls could listen to. The door was open. Our turn had arrived. Here we are now. Entertain us.

Now we lived in a world of Grunge Gunk, where the bands we loved had a chance to get popular, or half-popular, or at least popular enough to get to keep making music, which is all most of them asked for. One night, before a special Seattle episode of *Cops*, the announcer said, "Tonight . . . in the city that gave us Pearl Jam . . . the cops are taking out the grunge!" Pathetic? Depressing? No. Awesome, we decided. Why not? We were easily amused. Maybe it was all the nail-polish fumes, but we were buzzing with energy. Our apartment flooded, so we just moved to the couch. For dinner, we cut across the train tracks to Wayside's Fried Chicken. On weekends, Renée and I drove out to the Fork Union drive-in to see cinematic masterpieces like *The Crush* and *Sliver*. MTV spent the whole summer blasting the video where Snoop Doggy Dogg wore his "LBC" baseball hat. Renée asked, "Snoop went to Liberty Baptist College?"

We both had raging crushes, which we loved to dish about together. Our big summer crushes were a couple of rookie grad students in the English department, named River and Sherilyn after the movie stars they reminded us of. Thank God neither of us was the jealous type, or the insecure type, or for that matter the cheatin' type, since sharing our crushes was one of the major perks of being married. Renée would catalogue my crushes. There was Bassist Cleavage Girl (from the Luscious Jackson videos), Tremble-Mouth Girl (Winona Ryder), Mick Jagger Elastica Girl (Angelina Jolie in *Hackers*), Painted on a World War II Bomber Girl (Jennifer Connelly), My Eyes Are So Big You Could Fuck Them Girl (Susanna Hoffs), and Madonna (Madonna). She introduced me to her own seraglio, from the Braves' Javy Lopez ("He sure is put together nice") to Evan Dando ("He must get more cookie than the Keebler elves").

At first, being married made me feel older, but that summer it made me feel younger, just because I had a wife I could count on to make friends for me. Her girlfriends became my girl-friends. I didn't have to do the work of scrounging my own social life because Renée pimped me out. She took me to parties and sent me to circulate among her crushes and pump them for information. At every party we went to, we'd split up at the door and work separate sides of the room. We had the system down: I was to check on her every forty minutes or so, touch her arm, ask if she needed a drink, and then she'd go back to work. On the way home, we'd ask each other, "What did he/she say about me?" River and Sherilyn came to our Fourth of July party, and it turned out Sherilyn was kind of a pyro, so she brought fireworks to set off in the citronella torches. We made mint juleps and had a blast. Renée got a wax burn while blowing out the torches and kept the scar the rest of the summer.

Every party that summer ended the same way: One of the girls would put on Liz Phair's *Exile in Guyville* and all the girls would gather on the back porch and sing along with the whole album, word for word, while the boys stood around in the kitchen and listened. It was scary, like the summer after sixth grade, when the girls back home would gather on the stoop and do the same thing, except they were singing along to the *Grease* soundtrack. Same girls, same summer nights, just different songs. Liz Phair was asking, "Whatever happened to a boyfriend?" and I would think, Well, some of us turn into husbands, and then nobody writes songs about us except Carly Simon.

Renée played this particular mix tape one night when she was sewing. Sewing was her most private activity, or at least the most private one I was allowed to sit in on. For a long time, she needed me to vacate the house whenever it was time to sew. After a while, it was okay if I stayed around, as long as I read a book and kept quiet. I was glad she was sewing because it was good for her. I was more glad when I got to hang out and watch. Her brow would furrow and her eyes would concentrate. Her mind would wander places I'd never seen her go before.

By the night she popped in this tape to sew, she was so comfortable she let me hang out and listen while she worked. I'd never heard this one before. She made private tapes so she could sew or work out to them. (Working out never got to be the kind of thing she could do while I was around.) Of course, the private tapes probably had all the same songs she put on all her other tapes. One side of this mix is uptempo, so I assume she used it for dancing and jumping around; the other side is quiet, so I assume it was for meditating or bead-stringing or sewing or other solitary pursuits.

Renée got seriously into sewing that year. She basically stopped wearing any clothes she didn't make herself, except for her Clarins work uniform. None of her store-bought clothes looked good on her. She was getting bigger and wider—broader hips, fleshier thighs—and she couldn't find any clothes in stores that would come close to fitting her. She used to cry when she had to buy ugly clothes from stores like Fashion Beetle or Aunt Pretty Poodle's, which were her only choices in Charlottesville. So she just started making her own. Her sewing-machine corner of the living room filled up with piles and piles of fabric and patterns. She made a dress form of her body so she could design patterns that would fit her. She would go to the fabric store, sort through the boxes of patterns, and buy them so she could copy them into something that would fit her. She basically had one mod minidress that she made over and over. She couldn't do zippers yet, but that summer she finally learned to do buttons and buttonholes, so she started making all her own foxy shirts. She sewed bike shorts to wear under her dresses so her thighs wouldn't chafe when they rubbed together. And she would come home with the strangest, sorriest fabric: pea pods, seashells, eggs, Queen Elizabeth smiling, anything.

The more pathetic and helpless the fabric looked on the rack, the more it would sucker her into trying to make it into a mod minidress.

The more she sewed, the easier it got for her to move and breathe, since she now had clothes she could move and breathe in, and feel totally hot while she did so. It was really intense to see how much control over her body she could have by taking control over her clothes. It took a lot of time to make them all, but she could sew for hours. While she worked she would lose all her nervous energy and glow like a conquering goddess.

She took me to the fabric store whenever she could. She said she liked to get my opinion about what looked cool and what didn't, but that was a total lie. She just liked having a boy to tote around the fabric store, and I knew it. I was always the only boy there, and she brandished me around the room like my grandmother used to whenever she took me to St. Andrew's with her. Or, for that matter, the way I did when I had Renée with me in a mildewy used-record store. I was a trophy, and I liked it. While she would pore over the giant books of patterns, I would ask the stupidest questions I could think of in a big, loud voice so she could show off how interested her boy was in sewing.

"Um, is that an empire waist?"

"Yes, Rob. Very good. That's an empire waist."

"I see. Why do they call it an empire waist?"

"It was invented during the Napoleonic empire." (I have no idea if this is true.)

"But Renée, explain this to me. Why is the waistline so high? Is that like a fitted boudoir?"

"I believe you mean a fitted bodice."

And so on. I would ask, she would explain. Boring. But I loved it and I knew she did, too, and I loved to pump up her vanity. Renée's vanity was a beautiful thing. I loved being her prop at the fabric store. In time, I started to love hanging around the store and exploring all the weird stuff they had there. To my fashion-illiterate mind, it was another planet. The signs they had up for fabric were a dizzying barrage of perfect names for new wave bands: Silk Shantung! Corduroy Remnants! Dalmatian-Print Fun Fur! That last one became the title of a mix tape. It also became a pair of pants.

Renée's sewing was a way for her to follow the changes in her body. She felt her hips growing more and more Appalachian, marking her as one of her people. She was starting to look like pictures of her late, beloved Mamaw back in West Virginia; sometimes this would make her uncles misty-eyed. Uncle Troy once gave her a hug and almost cried because the hug reminded him of Mamaw's body. Goldie Hughart Crist died when Renée was sixteen, but Renée felt like she was getting to know her grandmother better than ever now. There was a lot of history in the hips, and Renée was learning her history. With that sewing machine, she was making history of her own.

Around that time we went to Dublin (the one in Ireland, not the one in Pulaski County) to visit cousins of mine. As we walked down the street, she said, "You know, I'm starting to understand this whole Irish boy/southern girl thing."

"What do you mean?"

"I mean I have the only ass on this entire street. Look around."

"I've seen your ass before."

"Look at the men. The men are walking into walls."

"That's true. I thought they were staring at me."

"I have the only pair of hips as far as the eye can see. They have never seen a girl before. Holy shit!"

"I thought it was my new Suede T-shirt."

"None of these women have any ass at all. This is fucking awesome."

"It's a really cool Suede T-shirt."

"That last guy turned around three times."

And so on. It wasn't my Suede T-shirt, believe me.

The sewing built up her strength, that was for sure. She started writing down reminders to herself on an index card and kept it in her pocket all the time. The first line was, "Lots of people like me." She crossed out "Lots of" and wrote "Enough."

I'm very expressive.

I deserve to feel pretty.

I kissed the Blarney Stone.

I am strong. I am brave.

I'm a good friend. I am a good sister. I'm a good wife. I am a good in-law. I'm a good daughter. I am a good niece. I'm a good beagle mother. I am a good granddaughter.

I work hard for it, honey.

I'm Superfly TNT Motherfucker.

I'm pilot of the airwaves.

I'm a better third baseman than Brooks Robinson.

I B-E A-G-G-R-E-S-S-I-V-E.

I have exceptionally beautiful feet, eyes, ears, hips, hair, teeth, breasts, and shoulders. And fingernails. In a different pen, she added, And eyelashes and eyebrows, plus in yet another pen, And nose. And chin.

I never learned any sewing from Renée at all. That was totally her thing. But the intensity of her presence while she bent over the machine and made it hum—that stayed with me. So did all the pattern lingo and fabric jargon. Just more of that endless, useless knowledge you absorb when you're in a relationship, with no meaning or relevance outside of that relationship. When the relationship's gone, you're stuck knowing all this garbage. A couple of years after Renée died, I was in a room full of friends watching the BBC production of *Pride and Prejudice*. Everybody commented on those funny dresses Jennifer Ehle wears. "Mmmm, yes, the empire waist," I said. "Authentic to the period, but a daring choice, since it usually looks silly on somebody who isn't very tall. But she wears it well. Nicole Kidman wore one to the Oscars in 1996." All the heads in the room slowly turned and stared at me. I had no idea how any of this was stuck in my head. My friends waited in silence for some kind of explanation. Nobody was more curious than I was.

how i got that look

A PINK CHOCOLATE LIPSTICK	B LAMINATES AND MOLDING MUD
Liz Phair: "Supernova"	• Archers of Loaf: "Freezing Point"
Sebadoh: "Skull"	• Saint Etienne: "I Was Born on
Pavement: "Gold Soundz"	• Christmas Day"
Sugar: "Your Favorite Thing"	• Pavement: "Elevate Me Later"
Everything But the Girl: "We Walk the	• Sebadoh: "Rebound"
Same Line"	• Liz Phair: "Whip-Smart"
Hole: "Plump"	• Guided By Voices: "Gold Star for
Superchunk: "The First Part"	• Robot Boy"
Dinosaur Jr.: "Feel the Pain"	• Dinosaur Jr.: "I Don't Think So"
Frank Black: "Headache"	• Sugar: "Believe What You're Saying"
The Offspring: "Come Out and Play	• Rollerskate Skinny: "Bow
(Keep 'em Separated)"	• Hitch-Hiker"
Fuzzy: "Flashlight"	• The Grifters: "Cinnamon"
Stereolab: "Ping Pong"	• Sloan: "Coax Me"
Veruca Salt: "Seether"	• Weezer: "Undone (The Sweater Song)"
G. Love and Special Sauce: "Baby's	• The Wedding Present: "Yeah Yeah
Got Sauce"	• Yeah Yeah Yeah"
	• Palace Brothers: "All Is Grace"

The spring of 1994 was marked by two key events
in rock history: the death of Kurt Cobain and the birth of Zima.
In case you don't remember, and if you drank any Zima you

surely don't, it was a cheap, fizzy, clear, strong, thoroughly ran-
cid malt liquor marketed as a hipster "alternative" beer with
a shiny silver and black label that glowed in the dark. Let
me reiterate—it was cheap. One night, Renée started rummaging through the kitchen for mixers. She found a sampler box
of miniature liqueur bottles—an untouched Secret Santa gift
from a day job she'd had a couple years back—gathering dust on
our shelves and started trying out recipes to cut the toxic kick of
Zima. Cointreau was too bland. Frangelico was too nutty. But
then, one night, in a flash of inspiration that rivals the creative
energy of Chuck Berry the night he decided to mix country with
the blues, Renée poured in some sickly sweet purple syrup
called Chambord. With a little Chambord, a longneck of Zima
became a handful of flaming violet glass, a bottle that looked
like it could be set on fire and thrown at a bus or drunk with
equally destructive effects. One Zima-and-Chambord would
knock you on your ass; two would knock you on somebody
else's ass. It was the perfect rock cocktail.

It became our drink of choice for a long, lazy, rambling fever
dream of a summer, when Kurt was dead but the promise of
rock was raging on. The radio was playing hits by Hole and
Green Day and Weezer and Sugar and Veruca Salt. I would pick
Renée up after work at the Fashion Square Mall, then we would
go home and set up our wobbly little hibachi in the backyard,
grill some hot dogs, turn up the music, invite some friends over,
and start mixing the Zima-and-Chambord rocket capsules. To
this day, I still see that precise shade of purple sometimes—on

some jogger's track suit, or on some kid's Mylar birthday balloon—and it always triggers flashbacks that involve a throbbing headache and the cowbell solo in the Offspring's "Come Out and Play (Keep 'em Separated)."

Renée made "How I Got That Look" for those nights in the backyard. The title came from a monthly feature in one of her favorite glossy fashion mags, a feature that gave away the secrets of the supermodels. Side One was titled "Pink Chocolate Lipstick." Side Two was titled "Laminates and Molding Mud." Her big project that summer was her guitar. With a couple of her indie rock girlfriends, Katherine and Cindy, she started a band called Flirtation Device. Like all girl bands, they spent all their time thinking up cool band names and cool song titles and cool ideas for matching outfits, with only occasional efforts to actually play songs. When Cindy and Katherine had their big falling out over a b-o-y (what else), the band was history—but the songs on this tape still sound great, especially with a Zima-and-Chambord or two for audio enhancement.

Our town finally got an indie-rock club that summer. Tokyo Rose, the local sushi bar, started hosting shows in the basement. It was in a strip mall on 250 East, between the University Laundromat and the Pizza Hut. Our friend Darius talked the owner, Atsushi, into letting him book bands. The basement wasn't big, but it was friendly, with blue paint on the walls and loveseats you could fall asleep on if the band sucked. On a good night, Atsushi would close the sushi bar, come down with his acoustic guitar, and play his original Japanese ballads. He also sang some tunes in English, like "I Hate Charlottesville," which always ended up being a big sing-along. At the end of the evening, he would send everybody home with Roy Orbison's "Crying," sung in a falsetto that was wasabi on our hearts.

During this time, Renée quit the makeup counter to spend more time writing about music, and got another job at our favorite record store, Plan 9. Now that she didn't have to wear a uniform to work, every day was a fashion show. She was inspired to sew more than ever. She sewed her first zippers that summer, although she didn't really fully get the hang of them for a few months. She would park her Zima-and-Chambord on the window sill and concentrate on her patterns for hours at a time. She went to L.A. to do the *Spin* cover story on the band L7 and came back having learned all their makeup tips. Renée also took guitar lessons from a brunette named Mark. He was cute; otherwise, he wouldn't have been invited over to teach her guitar, since he was into terrible jam-bands. He played bass in a Phish cover band called David Bowie. But he was cute. She would make a pizza, he would teach her Beatles songs, and then he would ask her for girl advice. Renée coached him until he snagged a girlfriend, whereupon he couldn't come over anymore, since his girlfriend didn't approve of him hanging with a married woman.

The big crisis that summer came when the power went out for two weeks. We came back from a road trip and found the upstairs neighbors had skipped out on the Virginia Power bill. The phone was dead and most of the food in the fridge was spoiled. We had no hot water. We didn't have the cash to settle the bill and turn the lights back on, and we didn't know when we *would* have the cash. There was no way I could have seen it coming, yet the fact that I couldn't protect Renée from it drove me *crazy*. How could something like this just happen? Why couldn't I do anything about it? I had felt helpless many times, as an adult even, but feeling helpless as a husband was different from anything I'd ever felt in my life. This was just a temporary snag, but it made me realize how many more of these there were going to be. I was going to have to get used to feeling helpless if I was going to remain a husband. And being a husband made me helpless, because I had somebody to protect (somebody a little high-strung, who had a tough time emotionally with things like the lights going out indefinitely). Man, I thought it was tough being broke when I was single, but being broke as a husband is not even in the same category.

For two weeks, I lay awake at night and said Hail Marys over and over to stop my heart from beating too fast. I suddenly realized how much being a husband was about fear: fear of not being able to keep somebody safe, of not being able to protect somebody from all the bad stuff you want to protect them from. Knowing they have more tears in them than you will be able to keep them from crying. I realized that Renée had seen me fail, and that she was the person I was going to be failing in front of for the rest of my life. It was just a little failure, but it promised bigger failures to come. Additional ones, anyway. But that's who your wife is, the person you fail in front of. Love is so confusing; there's no peace of mind.

Every morning at that time, we went to Bodo's Bagels and split a three-cheese sesame. They always played a mix tape of Rolling Stones tunes there, and I found it immensely comforting. The first song was "Sittin' on a Fence," an acoustic ballad with Mick and Keith singing about how stupid people are for falling in love and settling down. I was amazed at how soothing their voices were, two brash and pretty young mod boys, harmonizing so confidently about how people who stay together are suckers, and laughing at them. And they're right—what could be scarier, stupider, than staying together? How else could you totally guarantee that you would always have reasons to be terrified? "Sittin' on a Fence," that was the life for Mick and Keith. (The crazy thing is, Mick and Keith are total hypocrites— they've been a married couple longer than my parents. If Keith really believed in "Sittin' on a Fence," he'd be Jeff Beck, who never gets trapped in a situation he doesn't control, and hasn't made a decent record since he quit the Yardbirds.)

I was still hanging on to grad school, but things were looking bad. The academic job market had crashed, leaving my whole generation stranded. I had failed in my duty to get Renée out of Charlottesville. She'd made a mistake trusting me. I snagged a job interview at the University of Southern Mississippi: adjunct, four comp sections a semester, for less money than we were making writing record reviews, in the same kind of college town we lived in now, except one where we didn't know a soul. It was a dismal gig, the academic equivalent of joining Team Hardee's, but it was our best shot. I didn't get the job and I got depressed.

I didn't want to talk about it.

"Refusal is not the act of a friend," she said. "You must let me draw the water from the well."

"Don't Barzini me."

"You didn't want that job anyway. I'd follow you anywhere, sweetie, but I wasn't dreaming about Hattiesburg, Mississippi. You don't have to promise me anything."

"We'll get out of this town someday."

"We like it here. We have each other."

"Someday."

"I grew up on country radio. You know I'm a sucker for that 'we got no money but we got love' crap."

"Someday," I said.

"Easy," she said. "We do not have to give assurances as if we were lawyers."

Kurt Cobain loomed over everything that summer. It's hard to explain, so let me rewind to the day his body was found. April 8 was the Friday of the weekend that the English department grad students were hosting a conference of our very own, titled "Cross/Roads and (Re) Mappings" or something like that, in true Judy Garland/Mickey Rooney "Hey kids, let's put on a show!" style. Our friends Ivan and Sarah were coming down from Brown to read a paper about Zizek. Meanwhile, we watched the coverage of Cobain's suicide on MTV. They were showing the *Unplugged* special over and over.

During that first week of April, spirits were high and hormones were in full rage mode. Charlottesville had a particularly huge load of pollen that spring, and I would walk home every day from teaching, kicking clumps of pollen around. The pollen was lush and green, so green it made me a little sick to breathe it in. Everybody was looking forward to having fun that weekend. The weird thing is, we *did* have fun. Everybody went to parties, brought their friends from out of town, drank a lot, gossiped about Kurt. Nobody was surprised, so nobody was depressed. People cracked jokes, even those of us who loved him. We improvised new lyrics to Nick Lowe's death ditty "Marie Provost" ("He was our Brando / He hung out with Evan Dando," etc.). Renée bummed cigarettes and poured Chambord into people's Zima bottles. News was exchanged jovially. Did you hear that the guy who found the body called the radio station before he called the cops? Did you hear he left a note? Renée and our friend Gina sang "Kurt Cobain" to the tune of "You're So Vain." For people who were into music, which meant almost everybody hanging around all weekend, the Kurt Cobain who finally kicked it was the celebrity, as opposed to the guy who had written all his songs and sung them—the musician. The celebrity was dead. The guy who sang on the *Unplugged* special was a little harder to bury.

This had to be the least surprising rock death ever. Kurt had been threatening suicide for so long that it amounted to playing a game of *Clue* with his fans. In Rome, with the pills? No, in Seattle, with the shotgun. *Saturday Night Live* was already doing "Kurt Cobain almost reached nirvana this week" jokes. He'd posed for more photos with guns than the paper had room to reprint. The Internet barely existed, as far as I was concerned, but it was already raging with a constant stream of Kurt death rumors. When the news arrived on Friday, it was like, Okay, whew, that's the last time we get this news.

Many of our friends reported similar reactions—one of my friends, who knew Kurt, was horrified to hear everybody making jokes within minutes of the body being found ("dead men do wear plaid"). Maybe people were relieved, or maybe they were venting their anger at how he'd abandoned them. All I know is how weird it seemed that Kurt provided the theme for such an intense weekend, one I knew I would always remember and always have. The pollen made the air smell sweet. Everybody looked good. The visitors from up north hadn't had a taste of the warm weather yet. My Boston buddies Ivan and Sarah had never met my friends in Charlottesville, and I got to show them off. The whole summer was going to be great like this, exactly like this. On Sunday, exhausted yet nowhere near hungover, even after sleeping on the kitchen floor all night, the four of us couldn't find any more Kurt on TV, so we watched *The Beastmaster*.

The celebrity death was a temporary rush of excitement. But the dead musician didn't go away, at least not for me. My favorite Nirvana song was "Heart-Shaped Box." I first heard it in our old

Chrysler, stopped at the red light between Cherry Avenue and the train tracks, on my way to pick Renée up from work, just as the sun was setting. As soon as I picked her up, I started trying to describe the song I'd just heard, and what it sounded like, and then after I gave up in frustration, we looked at each other and drove straight to the record store at the Seminole Shopping Center. (Note: the "record store" was a popular retail strategy in the 1990s, a building where people would "go" to "buy" "music.") We played *In Utero* all night long. Renée kept arguing that the melody of "Heart-Shaped Box" came straight from Blondie, and singing, "Hey, wait, I'm Francis Bean Cobain."

I liked *In Utero* a lot better than *Nevermind* because Kurt was singing about being a husband, which was both gauche and scary. It got under my skin. Singing about drugs and despair—no problem. Singing about lithium—kid stuff. But "Heart-Shaped Box" was about the fear of having somebody on your hands you refuse to let go of, and that was so new to me. I was terrified to hear somebody my age singing about it. On the *radio*.

The *Unplugged* music bothered me a lot. Contrary to what people said at the time, he didn't sound dead, or about to die, or anything like that. As far as I could tell, his voice was not just alive but raging to stay that way. And he sounded married. Married and buried, just like he says. People liked to claim his songs were all about the pressures of fame, but I guess they just weren't used to hearing rock stars sing love songs anymore, not even love songs as blatant as "All Apologies" or "Heart-Shaped

Box." And he sings, all through *Unplugged*, about the kind of love you can't leave until you die. The more he sang about this, the more his voice upset me. He made me think about death and marriage and a lot of things that I didn't want to think about at all. I would have been glad to push this music to the back of my brain, put some furniture in front of it so I couldn't see it, and wait thirty or forty years for it to rot so it wouldn't be there to scare me anymore. The married guy was a lot more disturbing to me than the dead junkie.

In *Unplugged*, Kurt begins with a wedding ("I doooo") and spends the rest of the show living out the promise, sinking his fangs into a lover who has married him and buried him. He's trapped inside her "Heart-Shaped Box." She's somebody he will never let go of, somebody whose cancer he'd eat to keep her alive, somebody he'll never leave no matter how toxic she gets. This woman might be named Mary, like in "All Apologies," or she might be named Anna Maria, like in "Come As You Are." Or she might even be named Courtney. Either way, he's stuck to her. He can't let go. Till death do them part.

First one of them will die, then the other one will. They don't know which one will go first, and it doesn't matter. Eventually, you're both dead, and then finally you'll be as one, in the sun, and then it's over, you're married and buried and nobody will ever see you again. Where *do* bad folks go when they die?

The show ends with another scary marriage ballad, "Where Did You Sleep Last Night," a song about a woman with a dead husband. Maybe she killed him, maybe she didn't—we don't know. But she can't sleep in her marriage bed anymore. Kurt has nowhere to rest, so he stays awake and shivers the whole night through. Just an hour ago, Kurt was singing "About a Girl," a groom singing "I do" over and over. But here he is alone, in the pines, in the pines, where the sun don't ever shine.

When you get married, you hope you die before your lover does. (Do they? Do people wish this consciously? Do they admit it if they do? Al Green sings about it in "Mimi," telling the girl he better die before she does because he couldn't take it; do people talk this way in real life?) I hoped it, but I sure never said so because I figured Renée hoped the same thing. I guess it's a long-term bet. When you get married, you make a plan to die, in a way. These thoughts had probably always been there somewhere in my brain. But I didn't like the way Nirvana made me brood over them. I hoped they'd go away. I didn't even tell Renée what an intense experience the Nirvana *Unplugged* always was for me—I thought that would make it worse, so I kept my mouth shut about it. I tried sittin' on a fence like Mick and Keith. It didn't really work.

I missed Kurt more the longer he stayed dead. He was one of very, very few male singers my age singing about love and marriage. The Notorious B.I.G. was really the only other one of his stature. Kurt and Biggie were the rock stars of my age who worried about the things I worried about, both of them in fucked-up marriages and yet writing songs about them that felt real. They gave me the sort of tiny wisdoms I got from surrogate older brothers like Al Green and John Doe and Lou Reed. They sang about morbid thoughts, about feeling ready to die, yet at least the way I heard their voices, they were fighting to stay alive. Maybe I'm wrong. *Definitely* I'm wrong; they're both gone.

But when I listen to Kurt, he's not ready to die, at least not in his music—the boy on *Unplugged* doesn't sound the same as the man who gave up on him. A boy is what he sounds like, turning his private pain into teenage news. He comes clean as a Bowie fan, up to his neck in Catholic guilt, a Major Tom trying to put his *Low* and his *Pin Ups* on the same album, by mixing up his favorite oldies with his own folk-mass confessionals. I hear a scruffy sloppy guitar boy trying to sing his life. I hear a teenage Jesus superstar on the radio with a song about a sunbeam, a song about a girl, flushed with the romance of punk rock. I hear the noise in his voice, and I hear a boy trying to scare the darkness away. I wish I could hear what happened next, but nothing did.

52 girls on film

MAY 1995

A SIDE ONE: WE ARE THE GIRLS OF THE USA	B SIDE TWO: WE'RE THE DANDY HIGHWAYMEN
Adam Ant: "Strip"	Bow Wow Wow: "C30, C60,
Human League: "The Things That	C90, Go!"
Dreams Are Made Of"	Adam and the Ants: "Stand and
The B-52's: "52 Girls"	Deliver"
Yaz: "Situation"	The B-52's: "Legal Tender"
Orchestral Manoeuvres in the Dark:	Prince: "Delirious"
"Enola Gay"	Eurythmics: "Sex Crime (1984)"
Thompson Twins: "Hold Me Now"	ABC: "Be Near Me"
Duran Duran: "Girls on Film"	Mecano: "Me Cole En Una Fiesta"
Depeche Mode: "Just Can't Get	Peter Godwin: "Images of Heaven"
Enough"	Peter Schilling: "Major Tom (Coming
Ray Parker Jr.: "I Still Can't Get Over	Home)"
Loving You"	November Group: "The Popular Front"
Haircut 100: "Love Plus One"	Dead or Alive: "You Spin Me Round
Bow Wow Wow: "I Want Candy"	(Like a Record)"
The Waitresses: "I Know What Boys	The Comsat Angels: "Will You Stay
Like"	Tonight?"
Vanity 6: "Nasty Girl"	Kim Wilde: "Tuning In Turning On"
	Haysi Fantayzee: "Shiny Shiny"
	Dominatrix: "The Dominatrix Sleeps
	Tonight"
	Indeep: "Last Night a DJ Saved
	My Life"

Every time I have a crush on a woman, I have the same fantasy: I imagine the two of us as a synth-pop duo. No matter who she is, or how we meet, the synth-pop duo fantasy has to work, or the crush fizzles out. I have loads of other musical fantasies about my crushes—I picture us as a Gram-and-Emmylou country harmony duo, or as guitarists in a rock band, trading off vocals like Mick and Keith. But for me, it always comes back to the synth-pop duo. The girl is up front, swishing her skirt, tossing her hair, a saucy little firecracker. I'm the boy in the back, hidden behind my Roland JP8000 keyboard. She has all the courage and star power I lack. She sings our hit because I would never dare to get up and sing it myself. She moves the crowd while I lurk in the shadows, lavishing all my computer-blue love on her, punching the buttons that shower her in disco bliss and bathe her in the spotlight. I make her a star.

I am always fueled by my synth-pop fantasies. It's fun thinking up the names for these groups. These days I live a few blocks away from a store called Metropolitan Floors, which is the greatest synth-pop duo name ever, I think. I want to be in a band called Metropolitan Floors. (Never "the"—real synth-pop duos never have a "the" in their names.) According to the awning, "We're More Than Just Floors!" I actually stopped in Metropolitan Floors once to look around, before the guy started asking me what kind of carpet I wanted and whether I planned to lay it myself. I was unable to bluff, since "I want to build some 1982 synthesizers and learn to play them and attract a girl to be my lead singer so we can tour the world and make people dance and pretend to be German"—didn't seem plausible. I just took his business card and promised to call the next day.

I *always* pictured Renée and me in our synth-pop duo. I never told her about this. In my dreams, she tossed her fake-red locks and stood tall in expensive platforms. We had lots of band names: Multiplex. Metroform. Angela Dust. Unpleasant Pleasures. Schiaffiano. Criminally Vulva. Indulgence. Appliancenter. She never knew any of this.

It's odd that I've never pictured myself as a solo rock star. I've always dreamed of a new wave girl to stand up front and be shameless and lippy, to take the heat, teach me her tricks, teach me to be brave like her. I needed someone with a quicker wit than mine. The new wave girl was brazen and scarlet. She would take me under her wing and teach me to join the human race, the way Bananarama did with their "Shy Boy." She would pick me out and shake me up and turn me around, turn me into someone new. She would spin me right round, like a record.

It was a pipe dream—I could never play an instrument, not even a simple keyboard. In all my years of fiddling with keyboards, all I ever learned to play was "Way Down upon the Swanee River," and even that required playing the melody by numbers (3-2-1, 3-2-1, 8-6-8, 5-3-1-2, thank you good night). Operating synthesizers and sequencers was way beyond my skill set. But when I slipped into my fantasy world, I was bolder, juicier than I was in any facet of my real life. I would turn from cherry red to midnight blue, sixteen blue, blue blue electric blue. So I would daydream names and clothes and set lists for this band. I would pick out our songs, and make tapes of our greatest hits. The band name was one or two words; the album title was a pompous full sentence, like *I've Been Undressed by Kings* or *I Cannot See What Flowers Are at My Feet*. (There were even synthpop duos who picked *names* that were complete sentences, like Johnny Hates Jazz or Swing Out Sister or Curiosity Killed the Cat, but this is just trying too hard.) And of course, I would pick out a new wave girl singer. That was the whole point.

The boy-girl synth-pop duo is my favorite band lineup. Yaz were the ultimate. After Vince Clarke quit Depeche Mode, he went and found a new singer, Alison Moyet, who sounded like a *real person*—quite a breakthrough in new wave terms. They laid it out in the *Upstairs at Eric's* credits: "Alison Moyet—voice and piano. Vince Clarke—noises." They called one of their records *You and Me Both*—two kids conning the world together, a boy who needed a human touch and a girl who needed a cerebro-electro henchman. They made a strange pair: Vince tense and introverted, Alison loud and rude. And according to legend, they hated each other in real life. But it was fun to imagine that one night Alison had reached out a hand, smudged a little glitter on Vince's cheek, and left him never the same. You could hear it in the music, couldn't you? I could. And I'd listen to those records and think, Well, if it could happen to him, there's hope for all of us. Now she's in control, she's his lover. Nations stand against them, but he's her brother. She'll get to you somehow.

There were loads of new wave hitmakers who followed the same formula. Eurythmics were more famous than Yaz, though not as good (but I loved "Who's That Girl?" and "Sexcrime (1984)"). St. Etienne was one girl and two boys. Blondie had Debbie Harry and Chris Stein. Nena had a boy, I think. The Divinyls fit the format, even if the boy technically played guitar. The Pet Shop Boys worked wonders when they had a new wave girl singer up front, like Dusty Springfield ("What Have I Done to Deserve This?"), Patsy Kensit ("I'm Not Scared"), or Liza Minnelli ("Losing My Mind"). It's the perfect band lineup: You take simple elements—one boy, one girl—and use them to configure a whole pageant of sexual identities, dangerously mobile and dangerously musical.

The girl singer *means it*. She's *into it*. She didn't come for the finger food. Wherever she shows up—A song? Me? Well, if you insist—and before anyone can call security she's dancing on a table. She wants an amen, and she gets it. So many amens, so little time. The girl singer likes to wave her hand when she sings, wiggling spirit fingers or just raising a no-I-can't-go-on palm. Renée explained to me that this is a Southern Baptist thing. When you go to church, you raise your hand. It means you are testifying; you are under conviction. The new wave girl singer lifts her hand because she is giving witness to the spirit she feels, but she learned the move from other pop singers, not in church. Dusty Springfield always raised her hand whenever she sang. According to legend, she couldn't remember the words, so she wrote them on her sleeve. I love that story, Dusty raising her hand to read her little cheat sheet. John Lennon couldn't re-member lyrics either. But it's typical of Dusty's brilliance that she turned her dirty little secret into a flamboyant flutter.

Hardly any synth-poppers made it as functional romantic couples. The only one I can think of is the Thompson Twins, and they chose to keep it a secret—they probably never even told the other guy in the Thompson Twins. But that fantasy is there in the music, anyway. The reality of boy-girl life gets harsh, but in my fantasy, the music keeps them together. Even when we know the people in these bands hate each other in real life, we hear something different.

Take the Human League. Everybody knows "Don't You Want Me." Everybody loves this song. Nobody would remember it except for the girl who sings the second verse. It's some of the clumsiest singing ever smuggled into the Top 40, a common voice, a girl who has to be free and has no special reason to give, nothing clever to say. She's just speaking her piece, and not even taking any pleasure in that. Part of the joy of the Human League is Phil Oakey indulging his vocal melodrama—"dooon't! don't you waaant me!"—versus the dippy flatness of the girls in the band. They sing "(Keep Feeling) Fascination" and they can't keep a straight face. In the video, Phil is preening, seducing the camera, while the girls swing their hands back and forth, lock eyes, and know that teenage boys in America are watching closely to see their tongues flicker out when they pronounce the "l" in "love so strong." I know I waited for that moment every time.

It's a pop cliché that the ideal band partnership is between the guy who lives it and the guy who writes songs about it. Like the Stones: Keith Richards did all the drugs and broke all the laws and got busted in all the hotel rooms, providing raw material to inspire Mick Jagger, who wrote some of his best songs about how fucked-up Keith was. Or the Beach Boys: Dennis Wilson went surfing and hot-rodding and girl-chasing and around-getting, while Brian Wilson sat in his room writing songs about the fun he thought Dennis was having. (In reality, they were both pretty miserable.) Brian Wilson never went surfing in his life, but Dennis never could have written "I Get Around." Think of Johnny Thunders and David Johansen, Liam and Noel Gallagher, Bob Stinson and Paul Westerberg, Elton John and Bernie Taupin, Ray and Dave Davies, David Lee Roth and Eddie Van Halen. In a synth duo, this dynamic is right out front. One partner hides behind a bank of synthesizers and watches as the performer takes the stage. One *is* voice, celebrity, performance; the other *is* music.

The new wave girl knows what pop dreams are made of. She knows that Debbie Harry was just kidding when she sang, "Dreaming is free." She knows dreams are something you have to steal. The new wave girl scams on other people's identities, mixing and matching until she comes up with a style of her own, knowing that nothing belongs to her, that she just gets to wear it until somebody else comes along with faster fingers to snatch it away. She knows pop dreams are a hustle, a deception, a "glamour" in the witchcraft sense of the word. She knows how to bluff and how to scam. She sings about counterfeiting, shoplifting, bootlegging, home taping. She's in on the hustle— you steal it, it's yours, it's legal tender. The new wave girl knows all this, which is why she is dangerous. The new wave boy knows how dangerous she is, which is why he stands behind her.

The boy and the girl, together in electric dreams.

crazy feeling

A SIDE ONE DATE/TIME	**B** SIDE TWO DATE/TIME
Sleater-Kinney: "One More Hour"	• Peter Green's Fleetwood Mac:
David Bowie: "DJ"	• "Albatross," "Looking for
Bob Dylan: "If You Gotta Go, Go Now"	• Somebody," "Like Crying,"
Lou Reed: "Crazy Feeling"	• "Man of the World"
Lois: "Capital A"	• Bruce Springsteen: "Nebraska"
Roky Erickson: "You Don't Love Me Yet"	• Lou Reed: "A Gift"
Sleater-Kinney: "Little Babies"	• Yo La Tengo: "The Lie and How We
Leadbelly: "Rock Island Line"	• Told It"
The Softies: "Excellent"	• Steely Dan: "Barrytown"
The Softies: "The Best Days"	• Bob Dylan: "Highway 61 Revisited"
Morrissey: "Interesting Drug"	• Lou Reed: "Ooohhh Baby"
Lois featuring Elliott Smith: "Rougher"	• The Byrds: "You Won't Have to Cry"
Rolling Stones: "Dontcha Bother Me"	• Bob Dylan: "Tell Me Mama"
The Blow Monkeys: "Digging Your	• Lou Reed: "Coney Island Baby"
Scene"	•
Yo La Tengo: "Green Arrow"	•

May 11, 1997, was a lazy Sunday afternoon. Renée and I had spent the entire weekend lounging in the new summer sun, reading and listening to music. We spent Saturday night at home, just the two of us. She sent me to the bookstore and the fabric store with her shopping lists. After I got home with her loot—fashion mags, rock mags, Annie Proulx and Claire Messud novels—we sat on the couch eating Indian take-out and watching a terrible old Joan Collins/Richard Burton movie on AMC. It was called *Sea Wife*. Joan and Richard were stuck on a raft with two other guys after their ship sank. Richard was the only one who knew that Joan was secretly a nun, but she made him promise not to tell the others since the hope of sleeping with her was the only thing keeping them alive.

Renée assigned me to DJ duty while she sat at the sewing machine. We stayed up late that night playing CDs, mostly old favorites: R.E.M.'s *Murmur* and *Reckoning*, Liz Phair's *Exile in Guyville*, The Replacements' *Let It Be*, The Feelies' *Only Life*, *Marshall Crenshaw*. I remember the playlist because I left the pile of discs untouched on top of the stereo for weeks afterward. We listened to Freakwater's "Wild and Blue," Paul Revere and the Raiders' "Just Like Me," The Dream Syndicate's "Halloween," Everything But the Girl's *Amplified Heart*, Buddy Holly's *Greatest Hits*, Gregory Abbott's "Shake You Down," OMC's "How Bizarre." The top CD on the pile was the last one we played, Dean Martin's *Sleep Warm*, which stayed on continuous play as we drifted to sleep.

May 11 was Mother's Day, so we left phone messages for our moms. Renée did some more sewing and listened to the Baltimore Orioles playing the Seattle Mariners on TV. Joey Cora, her favorite Mariner, was having a good day. I was in the kitchen making lunch for Renée—cinnamon toast and coffee. Renée stood up, took a step, and then suddenly fell over onto the chair by her desk. I ran to her. I held her up with my arms and tried to talk to her. I grabbed the phone with my right hand, propping her up with my left arm.

"It's important that you remain calm," the 911 operator said.

The coroner later told me that she died instantly, that pulmonary embolisms kill in less than a minute, that even if it had happened in a hospital, the doctors would have been powerless to save her. But I was still propping her up, trying to breathe into her mouth while the 911 operator gave me instructions over the phone. When the ambulance came, the EMTs came into the living room and one of the cops led me outside. When the cop asked me questions about Renée, I figured he was gathering information for the hospital. I was worrying that she might have suffered harm from the oxygen deprivation. The officer and I were leaning on his car, out on Highland Avenue. Every minute or so, our next-door neighbor would peek over the fence. One of the EMTs came out to talk to me. "We're taking her to Richmond for the autopsy," she said. "It's standard procedure when somebody so young dies."

That was the first moment anyone said anything about Renée dying. It seemed like such a long time before I heard my stupid voice asking, "She died?" The sun was streaking through the leaves in the yard next door. The upstairs neighbors' air conditioner was right over my head, drip, drip, drip. The EMT said something about God, but she was just trying to be kind. Maybe it was a heart attack, she said; it was too soon to tell. I was sure they would find something in Richmond they hadn't found here, and I knew they would be bringing Renée back later that day.

The cops were extremely kind. They were young and scared husbands, like me. They wouldn't leave until I called somebody to come over. But I didn't want to call anybody because I didn't want to have to call them later and apologize for the false alarm; of course Renée would be coming back. I let the cops call St. Thomas, and they sent a young priest over right away. Renée and I knew him as the guy who'd given a sermon in which he mentioned the Primitive Radio Gods, which seemed at the time like a strange way for a young priest to try to be hip. He arrived in a polo shirt and khakis, just out of the shower, and he seemed annoyed to be there. I tried to make conversation but he had nothing to say, not even some drivel about God. I asked if he could give Renée extreme unction, and he said, "We can bless the body at the funeral," like I was too dumb to know the difference. Fortunately, it wasn't difficult to get rid of him. After a few minutes I told him I was okay, and he believed me. I needed to be alone.

Our living room was just the way the EMTs left it: The couch was pushed up against the bookcase, and there was medical debris all over the floor—yellow plastic caps, syringe wrappers, needles, styrofoam pads for the heart-jumper-cables. I was grateful that the room was so trashed because it offered visible proof that something bad was happening, that this wasn't just a bad dream. I cleared a little space and sat on the floor between

Renée's purple desk and her bureau—where her body had been—in the fetal position, my knees up, holding the phone.

I sat there alone for hours. I'm not sure how much time passed. It was maybe four in the afternoon, about an hour after Renée collapsed. Renée (unlike me) had a notebook in which she kept people's phone numbers, so I started there. Everybody I called was surprised to hear my voice on the phone in the middle of a Sunday afternoon. I simply told everybody, "I have bad news. Renée died." There was no way to tell people—nobody had seen her sick, nobody had had any idea she was about to die. Many of the friends and family I called had spoken to her within the past couple of days. It was Mother's Day, so both my mom and hers were expecting happy calls. Pavement was playing in New York that night, so most of our friends there were out at the show, and I couldn't reach them.

I didn't want to get up off the floor because I wanted to be there when Renée called and said she was coming home. People wanted to come over, but I told them to wait. Her parents, Buddy and Nadine, asked if they could come and get me, but I didn't want to leave the house, since I didn't want to miss the call from Richmond that would explain that it was all a mistake. I couldn't bear the idea of leaving the room where she died; I guess I must have known I couldn't get back in.

The sun set and the house grew dark. The call from Richmond didn't come. I have no idea how long I sat there. Finally, our friend Susan came over, even though I'd begged her not to.

Talking to her face-to-face, I realized that I had said something that could never be taken back—Renée died—and that saying it made it true. The change had come. It was irreversible. It was ten or eleven before I left the house. I packed the beagle in the car and drove to Pulaski County. I took the phone, even though it was a land line and would be totally useless in the car. But I couldn't stand to leave the phone behind, in that room. I thought if I left it there, Renée might call, trying to get back home, and she wouldn't be able to reach me, and I would have lost her for good.

It was a long drive, about three hours. I tried the radio only once, after the turn off of Route 646 onto the main drag in Christiansburg, a long string of truck stops and gas stations. The radio was playing "American Pie," but I only made it a few seconds before I had to change the station. I got Jerry Lee Lewis on the oldies station. He's still alive, I thought. Jerry Lee Lewis. Reagan is, too. The Pope. I turned off the radio and left it off. The beagle and I were both making a lot of noise, howling in our complete privacy. The signboard outside the Pulaski Baptist Church read NO MAN IS POOR WHO HAS A GODLY MOTHER.

The next few days were a blur. Less than twenty-four hours after I was making Renée's cinnamon toast, I was driving around Pulaski County with her parents, shopping for grave-sites. The saleslady wore a blue prom dress and carried smell-ing salts. She leaned on me hard to buy a grave for myself; I guess she thought it would seem romantic. I told her, No thanks, not today. She smirked a bit. "You're young now," she said. "A few years down the line, you'll be changing your tune, and that spot will be taken."

We found a spot for Renée on the side of a hill, in Sunrise Burial Park on Route 11. It was better than flat ground. You could hear the roar of the racetrack, just an exit away.

Now everybody knew it was true. I hated telling people because I thought I would have to apologize later for scaring them unnecessarily, but slowly it became obvious that the bad news wasn't going to change. Her family was so kind to me, although I felt ashamed that their daughter had died on my watch. Neighbors brought over trays of sausage biscuits. I picked out a casket (they show you a catalog) and wrote an obituary for the Roanoke paper. Friends were calling each other instead of hearing it from me. It was out of my hands. I stayed down the hall from her parents, in the room where she grew up. We'd stayed here many times as a couple. I lay there in the dark but didn't sleep, surrounded by her records, her photo albums, her Nancy Drew mysteries, her high school yearbooks, the model horses on her bureau.

Our friends and family converged on Pulaski County, even though it's an hour from the nearest airport and has hardly anywhere to stay. People who barely knew each other were squeezing into EconoLodge singles together. People drove hours to attend the wake, bringing me little things of hers to drop into the casket so she could be buried with them, *Beowulf*-style. Karl brought a guitar pick because he used to teach Renée guitar. Matt brought her batting gloves; they used to drive out to the batting cage in Richmond together, and he kept her gloves in his glove compartment. I lost track of how many people brought baseballs. Uncle Zennis's car broke down on the drive from South Carolina, which was a blessing in a way, since the uncles then got to spend the whole week in the yard working on a car together. It was just the distraction they needed, and I heard the comforting clank from the front yard all week long.

I wish I'd been together enough to organize a funeral, the kind of funeral people imagine when they say, "I want this song played at my funeral" or "Dress sexy at my funeral." But I wasn't. Renée was a gal with many fantasies, but as far as I knew she never spent her time fantasizing about funerals, which was one of the millions of things I loved about her. So I left it up to the preacher. I knew she had a favorite hymn ("Shall We Gather at the River") and a favorite psalm (the forty-third), so I mentioned those. My dad called around and found a Catholic monsignor in Roanoke. I went back to Charlottesville to pick out some glam burial clothes with Renée's sister, Drema, and her friend Merit. We spent an afternoon at our house picking out the shoes. We thought about the platform black-and-white creepers, but we decided to go instead with the pink patent leather pumps she'd bought at Fluevog in Boston. We picked out some jewelry and a green dress she'd sewn and some photos to put on the casket so people could see her the way she really looked in life. Drema checked Renée's speed-dial just to make sure she was number one. She was. Drema and Merit then drove me back to Pulaski County. On the way we talked about the road sign BRIDGE ICES BEFORE ROAD. I always wondered, If that's a problem, why don't they just build the bridge out of the same stuff they use to build the road? Drema explained that the bridge isn't made out of different material than the road, but that the bridge ices quicker because it's alone, hanging there without the land under it to keep it warm.

The funeral was Thursday afternoon, May 15, in Renée's old radio time-slot on WTJU. Nobody wanted to be there. My mom and dad sat in the pew right behind me and literally held me upright. During the funeral, I could hear a baby crying, which meant that our friend Heather had flown out from Utah with her month-old son, Eli. I counted ninety-six cars on the way to Sunrise Burial Park because I knew Renée would have counted. I was grateful for every pedestrian who took off his hat, everyone who sent flowers, every state trooper who saluted as the procession went by. We stood at the grave and listened to the cars on the racetrack make their noise.

After the service we all went to the basement of Fairlawn Baptist Church for lunch. It was a strange crowd: poker-night buddies, hometown pals, fellow baseball freaks. People sat with strangers, friends, enemies, exes, former coworkers, people they'd hoped they'd never have to run into again. They were all in one room, for the worst reason. I buzzed around the room, trying to take care of everybody; that's what Renée would have done.

We had come to say goodbye to Renée, but many of us were saying goodbye to each other. I didn't know which of our friends

I'd never see again. Neither did they. I caught a ride back to
Buddy and Nadine's with the two friends who'd hooked up at
our wedding, plus one of our groomsmen, plus Tyler, who got
carded when we stopped for cigarettes. We stayed around the
house all day, telling stories about Renée, arguing about the
things she liked to argue about. The uncles kept working on
the car in the front yard. Duane ran around to the neighboring
farms to roll in cow shit. The coroner called to explain how it
had happened. "Pulmonary embolism," he told me. "She never
knew what hit her." The coroner was very kind, and stayed on
the phone with me for forty-five minutes. I'd never heard of a
pulmonary embolism; he explained to me that a blood clot in
her leg broke off and got carried through her bloodstream to her
heart. I asked why. He said, "She was just unlucky." What can I
say? Renée was healthy. She was young. She didn't do drugs, not
even pot. She took zinc and used all-cotton organic tampons.
She walked the dog. She recycled glass. She wrote thank-you
notes and slowed down for yellow lights. She was planning to
live a long time. Still, she died, just because her blood stopped
working.

I drove back to Charlottesville with Duane. She was howling
because she knew that Renée wasn't going to be on the other
end of the drive. She was way ahead of me there. Stupidly, I
stopped at the grave the morning I was going back. I parked in
the Wal-Mart parking lot at the foot of the hill, bought a carton
of Camel Lights, and walked up to the Sunrise Burial Park.
There were no trees, no shade, just the widow boy standing on

the side of a hill, with a dog waiting in the car. The sun was shriveling me up, the air was draining out of my lungs, but there was nothing to see. She wasn't here. I couldn't have felt farther from her anywhere else. Duane and I drove away with nothing inside us. I talked to Duane a bit, kept repeating to her the line Harvey Keitel says to Tim Roth at the end of *Reservoir Dogs*: It looks like we're gonna have to do a little time.

It was high noon, and I remember it all—the nausea, the dizziness, the way my head felt like it was melting in the heat. I pulled off at a gas station in Syria, a small town near the Natural Bridge, and bought a souvenir shot glass. It was a Florida souvenir glass, with a big smiling yellow sun. We had always liked this town. It had a few junk shops, a Little League park, a movie theater. It was pronounced "sigh-REE-a," for the same reason Buena Vista was "BYOO-na-vih-sta" and Buchanan was "BUCK-cannon." I got back on 81 and tried the radio. Biggie's "Hypnotize" was comforting; George Jones's "He Stopped Loving Her Today" was too hard. I knew I would have to relearn how to listen to music, and that some of the music we'd loved together I'd never be able to hear again. Every time I started to cry, I remembered how Renée used to say real life was a bad country song, except bad country songs are believable and real life isn't. Everybody knows what it's like to drive while crying; feeling like a bad country song is part of why it sucks. There was an empty house on the other side of this drive, and I had no idea what it would be like to try to go inside it. There was nobody there. I wasn't driving back home—just back.

As I started to approach Afton Mountain, I heard a Prince song I'd never heard on the radio before, and I haven't since, either. "Adore" is a slow jam from 1987, the last song on *Sign 'O' the Times*, and I always thought of it as one of those Prince songs that should have been a hit. But it's over six minutes long, and there's no way to trim it down without losing the whole point. "Adore" might be the most beautiful make-out ballad ever—six minutes of erotic bliss that's more delfonic than The Stylistics and more stylistic than The Delfonics. I don't know why they played it. It was one of those lonesome stations you pick up between mountains when there's nothing else on the air, no mike breaks or commercials, just a song or two before the signal fades.

Prince was singing in his falsetto about heavenly angels crying tears of joy down on him and his lady. It was hard to hear. I pulled into a rest stop on 64 East, at mile 105 in Greenwood, on the side of the mountain. I parked and listened to the rest of the song, then got out and walked the dog. I sat on the trunk of the car in the sun and smoked a cigarette. It made me dizzy. I made my plans for the day. I was going all the way over the mountain, just another half-hour to Charlottesville. What would happen on the other side, I couldn't tell you.

I thought about this tape, *Crazy Feeling*, and wondered if I would play it when I got back. I kept hearing a song in my head, the first song on the tape, Sleater-Kinney's "One More Hour." I didn't know if I would play that song when I got back, or whether I'd ever want to hear it again. But ever since Renée died,

I'd been thinking about "One More Hour," the saddest Sleater-Kinney song ever. It was blaring in my mind all week, whether I was at the funeral home, or trying to sleep, or sitting on the floor waiting for Richmond to call and say it was all a mistake. It was all around and in my head, like the train rumble Al Pacino hears in *The Godfather* right before he shoots the Turk.

"One More Hour" is a punk-rock song where Corin Tucker sings about how she has to leave in one more hour. Once she leaves this room, she can't come back. She doesn't want to go, and she tries to talk her way out of it. But Carrie Brownstein sings to her in the background vocal, telling her it's over. The way their voices interact is like nothing else I've ever heard. Corin sings about walking out of a place she can never return to, leaving something she never wanted to let go, trying to haggle with someone who can't talk back. The guitars try to hold her in check, but she screams right through them, refusing to go quietly because it's already too late for a graceful exit. Corin snarls and she stalls, all for a little bit, just a little more time.

paramount hotel

JUNE 1997

A **SIDE ONE** DATE/TIME	B **SIDE TWO** DATE/TIME
Leonard Cohen: "Joan of Arc"	• Pavement: "Black Out," "Father to a
Pavement: "AT&T"	• Sister of Thought," "Best Friend's
Frank Sinatra: "How About You?"	• Arm," "Fight This Generation,"
Divine Comedy: "Becoming More Like	• "Kennel District"
Alfie"	• Frank Sinatra: "Swingin' Down the
The Germs: "What We Do Is Secret"	• Lane"
The Rentals with Damon Albarn: "We	• April Stevens: "I Want a Lip"
Have a Technical"	• Arto Lindsay: "Clown"
The Softies: "Count to Ten"	• U2: "Staring at the Sun"
The Legendary Jim Ruiz Group: "My	• Gloria Ward: "Oh Honey"
Amsterdam"	• Leonard Cohen: "Avalanche"
Tindersticks: "Dancing"	• Roxy Music: "Prairie Rose"
Julie London: "Daddy"	• Tindersticks with Isabella Rossellini:
Pavement: "Give It a Day"	• "Marriage Made in Heaven"
Blondie: "(I'm Always Touched) By	• Frank Sinatra: "Too Marvelous for
Your Presence Dear"	• Words"
Leonard Cohen: "Famous Blue Raincoat"	•
Smog: "Inspirational"	•

There *was a lot of music* that summer. I made tapes for the long nights when I would sit out all night in my backyard chair, smoking Camel Lights and listening to my

Walkman, staring out into the black woods at the edge of the backyard. I'd watch as deer with glowing eyes would tiptoe out of the woods, and then tiptoe back. Anything to keep from going back into my empty bed in our empty house.

My mix tapes were the life rafts that I held on to. I sat out there in the yard all night and listened to Frank Sinatra sing about waiting in vain, when the moon is on the wane, because he'd rather be swingin' down the lane with you. I would listen to the Germs scream L.A. punk noise about damaged kids sharing secret agonies nobody else can understand. I would listen to Bryan Ferry serenade his lonesome star in the sky.

I would listen and dream along. Sometimes I would sing to Renée; sometimes I would let her sing to me.

Sleep was the worst. I would lie in bed and my shins would ache, remembering how she used to kick them while she slept. Who knew shins had feelings, much less memories? I had no idea how to eat alone or sleep alone. I didn't know how to cook alone, go out alone, listen to music alone, shop for groceries alone. The things we used to do together were alien now. Lonesome star, shine on.

A few days after the funeral, a box arrived in the mail from New York's Chinatown. Inside was a bright green cuckoo clock, the old-fashioned kind with bells on top. On the dial were a couple of orange chickens. With each tick of the second hand, the big chicken would peck at the corn. Renée *definitely* picked this thing out. According to the credit card slip, she ordered it a few days before she died. She hadn't said a word about it to me.

I had no idea where it came from or why she wanted it. I put it up on her purple desk and let the orange chickens peck away.

I kept everything in the house exactly how Renée left it, so she could find her way back. I left her toothbrush hanging right by the sink. Her boxes of Kraft Macaroni & Cheese stayed on the same shelf where they'd always been. I didn't move a thing—her lipsticks, her cookbooks, her clothes, her shoes, the Pee Wee Herman bicycle she hadn't ridden once in all the time I'd known her. The pile of CDs we were listening to the night she died stayed right where it was. I wore her old Sonic Youth and Boss Hog T-shirts every day. I put my keys on her Guided By Voices bottle-opener key chain and used her Pavement ashtray. Sometimes I opened her sweater drawer to breathe in traces of her scent. I knew every time I opened the drawer, more of the scent would get lost for good. Duane kept scuffing over to her notebooks or her baseball glove, looking for any scent she could find.

At night, I would sometimes go out and drive in the mountains. I stayed out on the roads for hours, listening to Renée's old George Jones and Hank Williams tapes. Sometimes I'd go find roads we used to drive on together; other nights, I'd look for somewhere new. I had shrines and altars for her all over town, cruising around Route 33, "The Gateway To The Blue Ridge," or Waynesboro, where we went to the movies on our honeymoon. I decided to revisit the outlet mall where we got *The Best of the Best of Skeeter Davis*, so I just popped Skeeter Davis in the tape deck and let her guide me there. Now that I lived alone, I could do all the driving I wanted, and nobody would know or care. Renée's old country tapes kept me on the road. Hank Williams would sing all night about Jonah in the belly of the whale, Daniel in the lion's den, and how they tried to get along. If you don't try to get along, brother, you don't get another chance. Dear John, I sent your saddle home. I was looking for glimmers of light, but I only wanted to go looking for them in the hills where the dead spirits hung out.

I drove out to the 7-11 in Ruckersville to fill out a ballot for the baseball All-Star game. If Renée had had time to leave me a to-do list, I'm sure that would have made the top five. I cast her votes: Andruw Jones, Mo Vaughn, Joey Cora, Chipper Jones, A. Rod, Wade Boggs, Kenny Lofton, Brian Burks, Jose Canseco, Javy Lopez—all her faves. I knew Canseco wasn't a real All-Star, but I punched his box anyway because Renée always had such a massive crush on him. I completed her ballot and drove away.

When I had to go home, I would brew coffee and smoke cigarettes. I used to be such a great cook, but now I just ate chewy granola bars and peanut butter sandwiches. I was hungry all the time. I would drive to Arby's or Burger King and find a space in the parking lot and eat something hot and salty that would make me feel even hungrier when it was gone. I was surrounded by friends and family who wanted to help, but I was too frozen to admit how much I needed it, so I forced them to help on the sly. Friends sent me food, books, tapes. My cousins Joan and Mary sent me homemade blackberry jam from Alaska.

Whenever I got near the edge of sleep, my heart would race

and I'd bolt upright, hyperventilating. So I watched a lot of late-night TV, especially old movies about hit men and gangsters and pillowy dames. I watched movies starring Renée's favorite movie stars: Ava Gardner's cunning body, Rita Hayworth's hungry dumb flesh, Jane Russell's sullen sneer. I loved the scene in *The Killers* when Ava walks up to the piano in her black dress and sings her little torch song. "The more I know of love, the less I know it / The more I give to love, the more I owe it." Ava Gardner didn't lie.

When I fell asleep, I had dreams in which Renée was trying to find her way home, but she got lost because I'd moved a chair or something. In one dream, she was stranded in England after she joined the Spice Girls without telling me. (That is *so* something she would do.) She spent six months in Madrid, trying to get back to the United States, but she couldn't get a visa, and she cried for me to come and get her.

It made no sense for me to get morbid over Renée; she was the least morbid person I knew. Tragic, gaunt people bored her. She liked noise, she liked people, and she especially liked noisy people. She had no interest in death at all, so I stopped going to the grave because it made me feel too far away from her. God knows she didn't want to be there. I felt closer to her in Taco Bell—she loved the Choco Taco as much as she hated cemeteries. When I started feeling morbid and empty, I felt like I was turning into a different person from the guy she fell in love with. I had no voice to talk with because she was my whole language. Without her to talk to, there was nothing to say. I missed all our stupid jokes, our secrets. Now, we had a whole different language to learn, a new grammar of loss to conjugate: I lose, you lose, we lose; I have lost, you have lost, we have lost. Words I said out loud, every day, many times a day, for years and years—suddenly they were dust in my mouth.

Once, around supper time, I pulled over at a little general store in Crozet. I remembered this place—Renée and I went there one night, looking for a corkscrew, since we'd gone up into the hills with a bottle of red wine but hadn't brought anything to open it. How many years ago was that? Couldn't even guess. The guy didn't have a corkscrew, but he sold us a jackknife, and we did our best. I thought about going into the store and looking around, for old times' sake, but I didn't. I just killed the engine and sat there in the parking lot. I watched porch lights flicker in the hills around me. The headlights on the roads went dark, two by two, as everyone got where they were going. Soon the porch lights went dark, too.

mmmrob

A	"I SAW A SUB POP STICKER ON A SUBARU" SIDE	B	"PSYCHIC HEARTS GO OUT 2 U" SIDE
	Hanson: "MMMBop"	•	U2: "Mysterious Ways"
	Donny Osmond: "Last of the Red Hot Lovers"	•	The Breeders: "Fortunately Gone"
		•	Cibo Matto: "Spoon"
	The Osmonds: "The Honeybee Song"	•	Liz Phair: "Stratford-on-Guy"
	Urge Overkill: "Sister Havana"	•	R.E.M.: "Fall on Me"
	Donnie Iris: "Ah! Leah!"	•	Psychedelic Furs: "Highwire Days"
	Kiss: "Christine Sixteen"	•	Siouxsie and the Banshees: "Cities in
	Adam Ant: "Friend or Foe"	•	Dust"
	Heaven 17: "Temptation"	•	Luscious Jackson: "Deep Shag"
	Echo & the Bunnymen: "Seven Seas"	•	Soul Asylum: "Summer of Drugs"
	The Pixies: "Palace of the Brine"	•	The Who: "Drowned"
	Camper Van Beethoven: "The Humid Press of Days"	•	Thurston Moore: "Psychic Hearts"
		•	The Jam: "Start!"
	Talking Heads: "Houses in Motion"	•	R.E.M.: "Begin the Begin"
	Soul Coughing: "Blue Eyed Devil"	•	The Who: "Music Must Change"
	Stevie Wonder: "I Wish"	•	
	Skee-Lo: "The Tale of Mr. Morton"	•	

My friend Stephanie sent me this tape from San Francisco a few weeks after Renée died. She was totally obsessed with Hanson. Hanson's "MMMBop" and Missy Elliott's "The Rain (Supa Dupa Fly)" were the first new pop songs I loved that I couldn't share with Renée. She would have loved them both.

Stephanie, as you can tell, worships The Who. I do not, and we have been arguing about this for years. Stephanie once explained the plot of "Rael" to me, but I forgot it. As you can also probably tell, she has an extremely mod and generous new wave So Cal soul. She was a friend of ours in Charlottesville who split quick for the West Coast, but she was the coolest. She was the first friend I told when Renée and I got engaged. Her reply was, "It makes cosmic sense." She and Renée were tight. A few nights after the funeral, Stephanie called and told me about a crazy dream she'd had where all the dead people she had loved were riding bumper cars, and they were teaching Renée how to drive.

"If you're feeling happy vibes, they're from me," Stephanie told me after she mailed the tape. "I'm vibin' you real hard. I'm building a wall of love around you, three inches all around."

Did I mention that Stephanie went to Ridgemont High? She did. Her high school, Claremont in San Diego, was the school in the book, which later became the movie. She had Mr. Hand for history. I knew her for years before she ever brought this up, and I was pissed that she hadn't mentioned it before.

Hanson had such a cheery sound. Steph called them "Tony DeFranco for an Ani DiFranco world." Hearing Hanson segue into the Osmonds, I had to admit there was a cosmic connection there. I always had to fast-forward past the Soul Asylum song, but I listened to the Who songs a few times. (Steph labeled the tape with song titles on the front but no artist names, just to keep me from skipping the Who songs.)

I didn't know what to do without Renée. I didn't know what I was. I didn't have a noun. I was casually calling myself a widow, but was I really a widow? All the widows I knew were old people. I didn't know any young widows, and neither did anybody else. Nobody even had friend-of-a-friend stories. How could I be a thirty-one-year-old widow? I was a husband before any of my friends were, and just when I was getting used to the word "husband," what was I supposed to do with the word "widow"? After a few days, people started saying the word "widower." That was a surprise. Do people still say "widower"? Isn't that one of those archaic Victorian words, like "poetess" or "co-ed"? The verb is to be widowed, not to be widowered. I also once saw "widowed persons" in a book, but that was somehow even worse than "widower." I didn't know whether widowers existed, and I hoped we didn't since it was an even more brutal word than "widow."

All the songs on the radio started to sound like they were about Renée's death. I would hear the Radiohead song "Creep," and it sounded like Thom Yorke was singing, "I'm a creep, I'm a widow." Or I would hear Heart's "Crazy on You" and hear Ann Wilson whisper how last night she dreamed she was a widow beside a stream. Before Renée died, I always thought Radiohead was singing about a "weirdo" and Heart was dreaming of a "willow." Now, I could never go back to hearing them the way I heard them before.

The terrible thing about widows, is widows are terrible things. Their eyes are covered with sunglasses. Their fingers are covered with rings. They're jumpy, dumpy, frumpy, glumpy, dumb dumb dumb dumb dumb. But the most terrible thing about widows is I'm the only one. I'm the only one.

"Widow" was bad enough. Widow, widower, widowest. Widow's walk, widow's weeds. Grieving, merry, professional, peak, golf, grass, black. When copyeditors at the magazine need to cut a word at the end of a paragraph because it wastes a whole line, they call it a widow. But "widower" has that nagging "er" to remind you that you're not just a bereaved spouse, but a failed husband. You failed your wife by not saving her, or not dying along with her or before her. You're a widow with an asterisk.

I was ashamed to show my face anywhere, although my friends refused to let me disappear. Whenever I had to leave the house, I wore my wedding ring. I didn't know if widows were supposed to do that or not, so I just did it. I'd always been casual about wearing or not wearing it, but now I wore it every day. I would also wear my big Yoko shades. I always had thought of the widow's veil as a degrading medieval tradition, but now I realized it had a practical purpose because when you cry all day, your eyes become sticky and dust gets in them constantly.

There is so much about being a widow or widower that nobody tells you. There are no handbooks, and there aren't really role models. You learn a lot of useless knowledge you would rather not know. For one thing, the junk mail *never* stops. I am still amazed by this. It's been years since the funeral, and I am still getting junk mail and catalogs for Renée. It doesn't matter how much you call or write. It doesn't even matter how many times you change addresses. For example, today I got an envelope addressed to "Mr. and Mrs. Robert J. Sheffield," promising "Updated Information" from Pinelawn Memorial Park and Garden Mausoleums. There's a personalized letter, plus a leaflet titled, "Let's Face It Now." It reads:

Dear Friend,

There are a number of questions that every family must have the answers to. That's why Pinelawn Memorial Park wants you to have the information you need right now to provide your family with total protection and peace of mind.

The letter invites us to call for "our free family-planning booklet." Renée and I got a free family-planning booklet from the City of Charlottesville when we got married, but this is a different kind of family planning—junk mail from a cemetery. Who decided to send this to "Mr. and Mrs. Robert J. Sheffield"? Do they have any clue that the Mrs. is already in a cemetery? Or do they assume there is a new Mrs. by now? I'm impressed.

Another envelope came in the mail today, this one promising Renée "New Hope for Debt Consolidation!" Come on, give death some credit. At the very least, it takes care of your debt consolidation.

Another thing I learned as a widower is that you get a check from Social Security for $255. This is their way of paying back the decedent (another word I'd never used before) for all those years of work. I had to do an exit interview by phone with Social Security to confirm that the decedent had indeed died—it's required by law. They just wanted to check to make sure Renée didn't skip off to Brazil or anything. They were very nice on the phone.

The funeral cost $6,776.50. The guys at the funeral home were very cool about it; they said I could just pay it whenever I got the money, with no interest or anything like that. I sent it to them in checks, piece by piece, over the next year, until I paid it off. Copies of the death certificate from the State of Virginia cost $35 apiece. On my tax form, I checked the box, "Qualifying Widow(er)." I paid off Renée's credit cards after I paid off the funeral home. Her federal student loans were cancelled. Check this out: I sent Sallie Mae the check for her student loan on Friday, May 9, and they refunded the charge because they deposited the check on the following Monday, when she was no longer alive.

It is difficult to explain being widowed at the DMV, at the bank, at the post office. People get freaked out by it. Some people will give you a break, some won't. The very nice woman at the DMV let me re-register our car (it was in Renée's name) even though my copy of the death certificate was a Xerox because at that time I couldn't afford the $35 to order another. That was very kind of her. She didn't have to give me a break, but she did.

That was one of the strangest things I learned as a widower— how kind people can be. Renée's work kept coming out in magazines after she died, and people wrote in to these magazines to say that they were fans of hers. I remember a call I got about a year later, after Tammy Wynette died. I played a bunch of Tammy songs on my radio show that day, because honoring Tammy would have been Renée's beat at WTJU, and I wanted to take care of it for her. A total stranger, someone who just knew us from hearing our voices on the radio, called to say he liked the show. He said he was always a fan of Renée's show, and Renée would have been proud that I did right by Tammy. He also said that the next day was the Richmond Braves' home opener, and he was going to attend and think of Renée.

You lose a certain kind of innocence when you experience this type of kindness. You lose your right to be a jaded cynic. You can no longer go back through the looking glass and pretend not to know what you know about kindness. It's a defeat, in a way. One afternoon, I sat by Tonsler Park in Charlottesville and watched a Little League game and remembered my own days as a right fielder in the tall grass. I thought, None of these kids knows yet how much a coffin costs. None of these kids knows anything about funeral bills or the word "decedent." But there's a lot I know that I wouldn't give up. People kept showing me unreasonable kindness, inexplicable kindness, indefensible kindness. People were kind when they knew that nobody would ever notice, much less praise them for it. People were even kind when they knew I wouldn't appreciate it.

I had no idea how to live up to that kindness. There were so many people on the edges of Renée's life, and I didn't know how to take care of them. How do you tell her hair stylist? Her optometrist? Her shrink? The lady at the Barracks Road pizza place where we would hang out on Friday afternoons? I went back there often by myself, and saw recognition in her eyes, and heard curiosity in her "hello," but she never asked. Sometimes I was scared she would, or hoped she would.

What I wanted to do was simple: write notes to people, say thank you for making Renée's life better, you made her happier, you took care of her, I remember you for that, thanks. I got two of these notes written—one to her shrink and one to her massage therapist. And then I lay down on the floor and shut my eyes and thought, Well, that's enough of that. It knocked the wind out of me. I tried to say as many of Renée's goodbyes as I could, but damn, there was no way I could ever get her slate clean. She wasn't a person to tie up loose ends or settle scores. I wanted so much to write to Jean, her hair stylist at Bristles. She gave Renée three of her all-time top-four haircuts. She took care of the fake-redhead dirty work. She wrote out a list of Bette Davis's five best movies and told Renée how easy it was to get an annulment after we got hitched (well, thanks for *that* one). I wanted to explain why Renée wasn't calling anymore. Our friend Elizabeth, God bless her, wrote that note. I still have so many questions and regrets about all the people who knew Renée and enjoyed her and never got to hear the news from me, wondering what happened to that girl, why doesn't she come around anymore. To my great sorrow and shame.

I heard from the owner of the Meander Inn, the bed and breakfast in Nellysford where we spent our honeymoon. She saw Renée's name in the paper and sent me a card. What do you do with kindness like that? I felt tiny beside it, and stupid for not understanding the first thing about it. I had a lot to learn. It was bewildering and humbling to keep discovering how many brave things people can fail to talk themselves out of doing. There are a hundred excellent ways to talk yourself out of writing a note like the one she sent me, and I've used them all.

I even went to the bookstore and read Emily Post on the etiquette of thank-you notes. It said not to use the funeral home note cards, but to buy new stationery with black gilt around the edges and to use black ink. I got as far as the stationery store, but I didn't get out of there with any stationery because while I was browsing, I ran into my friend David, whose girlfriend was printing up some business cards. We talked for an hour. He said some nice things he'd been thinking about Renée lately. I drove home and crawled into my now-customary fetal position. I never got the stationery and left countless notes unwritten, again to my sorrow and shame.

I was helpless in trying to return people's kindness, but also helpless to resist it. Kindness is a scarier force than cruelty, that's for sure. Cruelty isn't that hard to understand. I had no trouble comprehending why the phone company wanted to screw me over; they just wanted to steal some money, it was nothing personal. That's the way of the world. It made me mad, but it didn't make me feel stupid. If anything, it flattered my intelligence. Accepting all that kindness, though, made me feel stupid.

Human benevolence is totally unfair. We don't live in a kind or generous world, yet we are kind and generous. We know the universe is out to burn us, and it gets us all the way it got Renée, but we don't burn each other, not always. We are kind people in an unkind world, to paraphrase Wallace Stevens. How do you pretend you don't know about it, after you see it? How do you go back to acting like you don't need it? How do you even the score and walk off a free man? You can't. I found myself forced to let go of all sorts of independence I thought I had, independence I had spent years trying to cultivate. That world was all gone, and now I was a supplicant, dependent on the mercy of other people's psychic hearts.

I was awed and ruined by this knowledge. Renée knew it all the time; I was learning it these days.

I played Stephanie's tape only in the daylight because I didn't want to ruin it by associating it with my nights. "The Rain (Supa Dupa Fly)" was for brooding alone at night, with Missy Elliott and Timbaland cheering each other up over those melancholy Tidewater swamp-funk beats. I couldn't believe both Hanson and Missy Elliott blew up at the same moment that Renée died; they were both made for Renée, and it was insane that she never got to hear them. Missy wrote a note to Biggie in her CD booklet: "Rest in peace, Big. I hope you can hear my album, wherever you rest." I felt the same way.

As usual, Charlottesville got a thunderstorm every afternoon that summer. I made a tape in which Missy's "The Rain" segued into Irma Thomas's "It's Raining," two of the saddest rain songs ever. Can you stand the rain? You say you can, but you don't know. I can't stand the rain. Counting every drop, about to blow my top. Falling on my head like a memory. I think I'll lose my mind, but not my memory. Missy babbles to keep herself awake at the wheel, making windshield-wiper noises with her mouth, singing "wikka wikka wikka," telling herself, "Oh, Missy, try to maintain."

I drove up to Boston for my wedding-anniversary weekend, since I couldn't stand being in the house alone. All the way up 95, the radio played an endless loop of Missy and Biggie and Puffy, "The Rain" into "Hypnotize" into "I'll Be Missing You" into "Mo Money Mo Problems"—all the current hits. The car was too battered to take it. My battery was running down. Every time I stopped for a traffic jam or a light, the engine stalled out and took up to half an hour to start again. I overheated on the D.C. Beltway, shifted into neutral, and tried to nose onto the shoulder. An old guy in a pickup jumped out and helped me push. He called a tow truck on his cell, but it didn't come, so I used my Kleenex pocket-pack to wipe the engine and then kept going.

Missy and Timbaland were still ruling the radio north of the Mason-Dixon line. When it actually started to rain, I held my breath and hit the lights. There was a thunderstorm at midnight on the George Washington Bridge, but Timbaland squooshed the bass in time with the wipers and pushed me to the other side. The river is deep and the river is wide. The funky drummer's on the other side. Every time I found "The Rain" on the radio, the bassline would pump for miles and miles. It felt like it was raining all over the world. Here comes the rain, here comes the wind, five six seven eight nine ten. Oh, Missy, try to maintain. And in an mmmbop you're gone.

hypnotize

OCTOBER 1997

A SIDE ONE DATE/TIME	**B** SIDE TWO DATE/TIME
White Town: "Your Woman"	· Janet Jackson: "Together Again"
Sugar Ray: "Fly"	· Scritti Politti: "Hypnotize"
The Cardigans: "Lovefool"	· Sugar Ray: "Danzig Needs a Hug"
The Notorious B.I.G.: "Hypnotize"	· The Notorious B.I.G.: "Fuck You
Meredith Brooks: "Bitch"	· Tonight"
OMC: "How Bizarre"	· Ghostface Killah: "All That I Got
Gina G: "Ooh Ahh . . . Just a Little	· Is You"
Bit"	· Billie Ray Martin: "Space Oasis"
Hed Boys: "Girls + Boys"	· Donna Summer: "On the Radio"
Grace: "Skin on Skin"	· Kristine W: "Sweet Mercy Me"
Air Supply: "Lost in Love"	· Daft Punk: "Around the World"
	· Erasure: "Victim of Love"
	· Donna Summer: "Dim All the Lights"
	· Serge Gainsbourg: "Ford Mustang"

It *was already cold before* the sun went down. Duane and I walked down Sunset Drive to the bottom of the hill and into the woods. We crossed the footbridge over the creek, past the farmlands, where we would see the cows laze in the sun. Usually, we turned around when we got to the path under the I-64 overpass, but this time we kept going for a few miles, all the

way down Green County Road, out to a stretch of Charlottesville I'd never seen before, not even in a car. Two-lane
blacktop, a Taco Bell, Hardee's, strip malls, and gas stations. We
didn't get home until around midnight. Duane went to sleep on
her rug. I sat in the yard and lit a cigarette. On the earphones,
Biggie was talking about a girl. They've been together a long
time, and she knows a lot of secrets about him she is never
going to tell anybody. Tonight, he's got something special
planned—he knows the kind of music she likes, that soft
Luther love-man Harveys Bristol Cream R&B shit, so for once
he wrote that kind of song for her, just to show he's listening.
"Fuck You Tonight" is full of mournful R&B chill but it also has
a cold-eyed gangsta pimp strut. Hail Biggie, full of grace, you
got a gun up in your waist, please don't shoot up the place.

I longed for a pimp strut of my own. Like Shaft, I'm a compli-
cated man and no one understands me but my woman, except
she's dead and she doesn't understand that any better than I do.

September had come and nothing had changed. I moved
into a new apartment, across from the Baptist church, one block
over from the Seventh Day Adventist church. But I had no
appetite to unpack the boxes, so I just left them on the floor and
stepped over them. It was more a shrine than a place to live in,
but at the time that's how I wanted it. Renée had never lived
there, and never would have consented to, since the bathroom
had barely any girlie storage at all and there was no counter
space in the kitchen. In my dreams, she came looking for me at
my old address and couldn't find me. A couple of times, Duane

ran away and showed up the next day at the old apartment, no doubt looking for Renée. The people who lived there now were very nice to her and called the landlord, who called me. At night, I sat in the same chair in a different backyard, staring all night into different woods, except nothing I saw there had any good news to tell me about the future.

A few days after I moved in, I was sitting in the yard and Mr. Kirby from next door came over to say hi. He was a widower, too. His first wife died of liver cancer in 1988, and a year and a half later, he married Mrs. Kirby, who came over the next day with some banana bread. They went to the Baptist church across the street. They were in their seventies. The boys who lived upstairs worked at the Higher Grounds coffee stand and played in one of our town's most popular underground funk-metal bands, Navel. All day, the guitarist would practice licks (Rage's "Killing in the Name" was a big favorite), and all night his brother the bassist, would have incredibly loud sex in the room above mine, to the point where I would get up and go sleep on the couch.

I had no idea until that year that Charlottesville could get so windy in October. I had never slept there alone in cold weather. Our old blankets were still packed in a box somewhere. While looking for them, I opened up a box of Renée's fabric, the fabric she left behind in the middle of her grandiose fashion designs. I pulled out massive sheets of red and blue corduroy and piled them on the bed for covers. There was plenty more of the corduroy (what the hell was she making, a sofa?) so I draped it over the windows to keep out the wind and the light. One red window, one blue window.

The way I pictured it, all this grief would be like a winter night when you're standing outside. You'll warm up once you get used to the cold. Except after you've been out there a while, you feel the warmth draining out of you and you realize the opposite is happening; you're getting colder and colder, as the body heat you brought outside with you seeps out of your skin. Instead of getting used to it, you get weaker the longer you endure it. I was trying so hard to be strong. I knew how to go out, how to stay in, how to get things done, but that was it.

Some nights I would drive up Route 29 to the all-night Wal-Mart. I'd push a cart around with some paper towels inside to look like a real shopper, just to spy on married people. I just wanted to be near them, to listen to them argue. This one is $2.99! But this one is $1.49 for just one! But $2.99 is cheaper per roll! But $1.49 is cheaper than $2.99! But we can store the other one! We live in a house, not a spare-towel storage unit, and we'll pay more than $1.49 rent on the space it takes to store it! But you can never have too much of it! And so on. Married people fight over some dumb shit when they think there aren't any widowers eavesdropping. And they never think there are widowers eavesdropping.

The Wal-Mart was always full of couples taking care of business. None of them were happy to be there, but they were there together, and I tried not to get caught staring while I followed them around from aisle to aisle. I was so hungry for the company. I was scared I would be caught, that my wedding ring would be put under a scanner and exposed as a fraud, a widower trying to pass as a husband. The store would start to empty around two in the morning, but I would often stay later. I was never the only person there, just the only man alone. I would look busy browsing the racks of two- or three-dollar cassettes: line-dance country, Christian anthologies, hit collections by groups like Three Dog Night or Air Supply.

Lots of the couples were younger than Renée and me. Some looked angry; others seemed comfortable. Sometimes I wondered if they were scared, the way I used to get scared when I was young and married. I sometimes wondered if they noticed me and wondered why the hell I didn't have a place to go instead of rolling a cart around under those fluorescent lights. But nobody ever noticed me. I never felt like going back home.

I ate a lot of widower food: peanut butter sandwiches, cereal, frozen steak burritos. I heated the burritos in the oven, and if they didn't come out thoroughly defrosted I said, Hell, what's the difference, and crunched through the frost. The hungry feeling and the lonely feeling merged until it was hard to tell them apart. I stopped cooking. Couldn't stand the idea of it. Who would eat it? Who would notice? Who would care? I gave away all of Renée's kitchen stuff, her cookbooks, her fancy knives, her chop dishes, her KitchenAid mixer. But there's still hunger. The sun goes down and there are quick decisions to make. Everything in Charlottesville closes by nine o'clock. If you live in a small town, and you aren't cooking, you're going hungry for a while. The restaurants where you used to eat together? Write them off. It's like they closed. I stopped going to the College Inn for pancakes because I knew I would see Gail, a waitress there who doted on us, and I never felt like having that conversation. So I went to the Tavern. Except Gail was a waitress there now, and she came over to pour me some coffee. She asked, "Where's the girl with the red hair?" I told her. Gail cried and said, "God takes the good people first." I couldn't go back there anymore, either.

I started going to Applebee's, a chain restaurant where I was guaranteed not to see any of my friends. I would sit in a booth with a book and be left alone, eating a steak and getting soda refills and eavesdropping on people who belonged to each other. I became a connoisseur of volume-oriented family-identified chain restaurants—the cheesier the better, especially ones with themes such as the Wild West or the Australian desert, where all the steaks would be named after resort cities and the baked potatoes would all have names like Uncle Stuffy's Baco-Blaster Cheddar-Chernobyl Twicersplosion. I knew I would be anonymous there, a guy nobody would notice or feel sorry for because the booths were too private and people had their own families to keep a lid on. The waitresses would be nice to me because I had no kids and therefore gave them no trouble aside from my unreasonable soda-refill desires. It was always hard to make myself go, especially facing that table-for-one moment, bluffing like it was a perfectly ordinary request. I had to be mighty hungry before I would even try, and more than once I got all the way to the parking lot and turned around.

Applebee's was my fave because the booths had the highest walls. Ruby Tuesday had better steaks, but the walls between the booths were too low, which meant a potential eye-contact issue. Outback Steakhouse also had short walls, but they turned the lights down low so it didn't matter. They blasted the air-conditioning to move people in and out fast, so I brought a sweater. I didn't have to worry about being spotted as a regular, because nobody worked at those places long—I don't think I ever had the same waitress twice. They were always cool about letting me stay and read. Sometimes I'd get static from the high school kid at the door. Maybe one time out of five, they would ask, "Do you mind eating at the bar?" But I never ate at the bar because once I said okay I would always have to say okay.

I still bought women's magazines at the grocery store, trying to pass as a husband shopping for a wife at home instead of a man living alone with a shopping cart full of two dozen frozen steak burritos. I hated living in a man's house, with a man's refrigerator and a man's bathroom. A man-woman bathroom only takes a couple of weeks to become a man's bathroom when the woman is no longer there. What a demotion: exiled to a bachelor pad. You know the Johnny Paycheck song "The Feminine Touch," or the George Jones song "Things Have Gone to Pieces"? Another thing only country singers understand. One day, you're in a physical landscape you share with this bizarre and fundamentally alien creature, not alien because she's female but alien because you're a fool in love and there's nothing not alien about that. And then when she's gone, you're alone and all the strangeness and wonder have gone out of the landscape and you're still a fool but now nobody notices how many days in a row you wear the same socks and cleaning the shower doesn't make the girl smile anymore so everything smells a little worse and doesn't get fixed when it breaks. Like Johnny Paycheck, I missed the feminine touch—not just hers, but mine. I missed being half-girl, half-boy, part of a whole. Now that I was male in a male environment, it was harder to manifest her physical chick presence, no matter how many of her MAC lipsticks I set out on the coffee table in a basket like so many M&Ms.

When my refrigerator broke down, I didn't call the landlord to replace it. I tried to fix it myself, enraged that my male fridge was giving me attitude. I lived on peanut butter and warm ginger ale for a whole month before I finally caved and called the landlord. I took out the champagne bottle, the one from the old house, the one Renée always kept around because she believed in always having a spare bottle of champagne in the fridge. Now it was warm and probably about to explode. I was too terrified to dispose of the champagne in a rational way, so I put on protective shades, wrapped up the bottle in Renée's old Motörhead T-shirt, and slowly dragged it through the yard and into the woods. I planned to go back and smash the bottle with a rock, rendering it harmless, but I could never find it again. For all I know, the champagne's still out there in the woods, waiting for the right moment to blow up.

It was hard to explain to my friends what was happening. When my friends and family would ask how I was doing, I stalled or stuttered or lied. Sometimes I could feel the glaciers shifting inside me, and I hoped they were melting, but they were just making themselves comfortable. All these monstrous contortions in me were warping the outside of my body, I was sure. No doubt people could spot me a block away and know that I had lived past my till-death-do-you-part date.

Sometimes I could hear my voice approaching the level of the Elizabeth Taylor mad scene. You know how in all the really great Elizabeth Taylor movies, the gnarly-ass melodramas, there's always the scene where she freaks out because she's living inside a horrible secret she can't explain?

Liz in *Butterfield 8*: "You don't know this. Nobody knows this."

Liz in *Suddenly, Last Summer*: "This you won't believe. Nobody, nobody, nobody could believe it."

I love Liz Taylor. Renée and I had a favorite Liz movie, *Conspirator*, where she's married to Robert Taylor, who's living a secret double life as a Soviet spy. At the end of the movie she's a widow because her husband has just been shot dead by agents of the free world. One of the agents explains to Liz that none of this ever happened, that for reasons of national security her widow-hood is a secret she can never tell. Then, I guess, she's supposed to go back to her family and invent a cover story about where her husband is. I don't know. The movie just ends with Liz getting told that nobody can ever know what happened to her and her husband. Nobody would believe her anyway.

jackie blue

FEBRUARY 1998

A SIDE ONE DATE/TIME	**B** SIDE TWO DATE/TIME
Queen: "You're My Best Friend"	Ernest Tubb: "Let's Say Goodbye Like
TLC: "Red Light Special"	We Said Hello"
Neil Young: "Field of Opportunity"	The Rolling Stones: "Connection"
Ray Charles: "Carryin' the Load"	Lefty Frizzell: "Long Black Veil"
Sonny Boy Williamson: "Don't Start	Bob Dylan: "You're Gonna Make Me
Me to Talkin'"	Lonesome When You Go"
Wanda Jackson: "Hot Dog! That Made	Johnny Thunders: "You Can't Put Your
Him Mad"	Arms Around a Memory"
The Ramones: "Questioningly"	Aretha Franklin: "Since You've Been
The Pooh Sticks: "Emergency"	Gone (Sweet Sweet Baby)"
Hanson: "Weird"	Elvis Presley: "Trying to Get to You"
Don Covay: "Watching the Late Late	Johnny Cash: "I Still Miss Someone"
Show"	Little Willie John: "Need Your Love
Tony Joe White: "Polk Salad Annie"	So Bad"
Hank Williams: "There's a Tear in My	Jimmy Wakely: "Walking the Sidewalks
Beer"	of Shame"
Touissaint McCall: "Nothing Takes the	The Monkees: "What Am I Doing
Place of You"	Hangin' 'Round"
Tavares: "That's the Sound That Lonely	Rod Stewart: "Mandolin Wind"
Makes"	The Rolling Stones: "Moonlight Mile"
Ozark Mountain Daredevils: "Jackie	Jacqueline Kennedy: "TV Address
Blue"	1963"

On the plane to New York, where I was to inter-
view some bands for *Rolling Stone*, I heard the two middle-aged
women behind me getting acquainted. One was traveling to her
son-in-law's wedding. Her daughter had died of cancer six
months earlier. The other woman asked, "Don't you feel strange
that he's remarrying?" The mother-in-law said, "No, Manny is
the kind of person who needs to be married. When she was sick,
my daughter said, 'Manny will be married again before dinner.'"

While I was in the city, I found an album at a record store in
the East Village. It was a Jackie Kennedy documentary LP called
Portrait of a Valiant Lady, rushed out right after the assassination.
According to the back cover, this was "an inspiring documentary
record specially written and produced for the listening pleasure of all Americans," put together by something called the
Research Craft Corporation, in association with the Bureau of
Auditory Education. Both sides of the album are devoted to a
biography of Jackie, "tragic heroine and First Lady of the World."
It has spoken-word tributes, a poem written especially for this
record, cheesy re-created versions of news sound bites, and the
voice of Jackie herself, from a TV address she gave around
Christmas 1963, saying thank you to the world for their con-
dolences.

I couldn't stop staring at Jackie's face on the front of the
album. The whole album cover is just one big photo of Jackie,
with no text or decoration. I don't know when this picture was

taken, before or after November 22. She sits pensively on a white couch, facing the camera with a sad little smile. She's wearing white. Her outfit is casual, maybe the top half of a dress seen from the waist up, maybe a sweater, with a discreet collar. She wears no jewelry. She's in a living room—hers? somebody else's? the White House?—with a lamp turned on behind her, on a coffee table laden with photos (too blurred to tell who's in them) and an ashtray. She's turned to the camera, as if we just interrupted her while she was staring out the window. The curtains are billowy and white. She rests her chin on her right hand, her elbow propped on the couch. Her left arm is casually draped over the top of the couch, and her left hand is hidden in the curtains.

You can't see whether she's wearing her wedding ring or not.

After I found this record I played it constantly. The Jackie bio follows her life story, as the narrator harps on the theme of her nobility with purple prose like, "She keeps a loyal, lonely vigil with his world." Her "Thank You" message on side two is really strange. The words are articulate, but her voice sounds shell-shocked. She seems to wander from the script, at one point pausing mid-sentence to say, "All his bright light gone from the world." It's a little scary to hear. Jackie apologizes for not answering condolence letters. For some reason, that's the main theme of the minute or so she speaks. She explains that she's gotten 800,000 letters. "Whenever I can bear to, I read them," she says. "It is my greatest wish that all these letters be acknowledged. They will be. But it will take time."

I wonder if all widows are obsessed with Jacqueline Kennedy. Probably. Renée and I were always obsessed with her, long before we knew either of us would be a widow. We were Jackies-ploitation junkies, poring over every biography, no matter how trashy. Renée, of course, already had a fetish for 1960s fashion (she even owned a vintage pink pillbox hat, which smelled bad enough to trigger her asthma), and I'm sure the obsession just got worse after she married into an Irish Catholic family. We looked down on people who called her Jackie O—they did not understand Jackie Kennedy, the Profile in Cleavage, the most bouviescent of all American Catholic girls. We watched Jaclyn Smith (the Charliest Angel) in *Jacqueline Bouvier Kennedy*, but we preferred Jacqueline Bisset in *The Greek Tycoon*. Once, when we were driving up to Boston, Renée made me drive hours out of our way down Route 3 to Hyannis, just because she was determined to buy some Jackie shades and a Jackie scarf to tie around her head. I assured her that Hyannis was literally the last place on earth Jacqueline Kennedy would have considered buying clothes, as it's a skanky little burnout beach town. But there was no way to talk her out of it. We got to Hyannis and hit the 99-cent stores. I don't know how, but Renée found exactly the shades and scarf she had imagined. The sunglasses were pointy at the edges; the scarf was multicolored and mod. She wore them the whole drive back to Boston, all three hours, tying the scarf around her head and making tragic faces out the window.

Jackie's the most famous widow ever, young or old. She's our Elvis, our Muhammed Ali. I was obsessive about her before, but now I was over the edge. I kept playing the first Pogues album, *Red Roses for Me*, just because of the album title—Jackie once said that those were the last words to cross her mind in Dallas before the shots, looking out at people in the crowd holding roses and thinking, "How funny, red roses for me."

People remember her—well, let's stop right there. Most of us weren't born then. We don't "remember" her, and we aren't even picking up secondhand memories from older folks who *were* there. We invent our own memories of her based on tokens like the Air Force One photo with the bloody dress, the funeral salute, and so on, including the documentary record I found. For lots of people, Jackie is a symbol of poise in the middle of grief, and since she was thirty-four at the time, she's also a symbol of youth. It's weird how you sometimes hear divorced people complain that they'd rather be widowed. It's not fun to hear people say this, if you're a widow, but I don't want to be judgmental about that—love dies in many different ways, and it's natural for the grass to seem greener on the other side. But it's not a competition; there's plenty of pain to go around. These people just don't know—and why should they?—that widowhood is not dignified, but degrading enough to strip away every bit of dignity you ever kidded yourself you had, and that in her time Jacqueline Kennedy made a fool of herself in public over and over. People project all sorts of strength and dignity onto her, but she was a mess, which is part of why I worship her.

Jackie wouldn't move out of the White House for two weeks after the assassination. It's an incident that's totally forgotten now, but it was a national scandal at the time. The Johnsons were trying to assume control of the White House, taking on their roles as President and First Lady, but they had to deal with the widow refusing to move out of her old room. They couldn't very well kick her out, even when Harry Truman was on the phone to LBJ, telling him he needed to get rid of her and claim his own goddamn White House. Lady Bird was a champ about it, saying, "I wish to God I could serve Mrs. Kennedy's comfort; I can at least serve her convenience." But Jackie wouldn't go. Two weeks! Not very "together" of her, now was it? Perhaps she knew she was being rude; she wasn't born in a barn. But she did it anyway. She overstepped the boundaries of manners, dignity, taste, and basic human kindness, because what else could she do? Where was she going to go? How would she get there? Where would she take her kids? How would she find a new place to live? How could she pay for it? She had so many decisions to make and no time to make them. This one she blew. History has forgotten, but it's one of my most cherished Jackie moments.

Jackie blew lots of other decisions, too, depending on which shady bios you believe. Did she sleep with her Secret Service agent? Did she sleep with Bobby, Sinatra, Brando, or the architect designing the JFK library? If she didn't, why the hell not? Wouldn't you? Did Ethel invite Angie Dickinson to sit in the front row at RFK's funeral just to get back at Jackie for holding hands with Bobby at JFK's funeral, since JFK slept with Angie on the night of his inauguration? Apparently, during the first few months, Jackie drank herself to sleep. Which means . . . what?

She got to sleep? Fair play to her. I tried drinking myself to sleep, too, but it didn't work. All it did was make me drunk, listening to the *clink, clink* of my ice cubes as they melted. Being drunk was a drag, but I liked the *clink, clink* and hoped enough bourbon would get the job done, so I drank a lot. Bourbon made me miss Renée bad, though, so I switched to Bushmills, but I still missed drinking with Renée and I still stayed awake.

The Jackie documentary record begins with the narrator announcing, "On Friday, November 22, 1963, at 12:25 P.M., Jacqueline Bouvier Kennedy began an ordeal unparalleled in human history!" It's a low-budget quickie for sure, with the same actor doing the same accents for the Indian and African ambassadors. A French voice proclaims her "charmante!," with accordion in the background. Somebody recites a poem ("The awful scream of the assassin's gun / Widowed her for life") in which "prayer" rhymes with "Bouvier." The LP covers the eighty-hour rush from Friday afternoon, when the assassination happened, to Monday afternoon, when the funeral was over and the story ends. In this version of the story, the funeral is the happy ending: "Never before has such a grueling ordeal been faced with such grace and poise as Jackie Kennedy displayed throughout the tragic circumstances so abruptly and atrociously thrust upon her."

I came to cherish this as a rock-and-roll record, as Jackie Kennedy's debut album, the greatest hit of a spectacularly fucked up sixties pop star. I realize she did not "release" this album. She did not authorize it, produce it, endorse it, or anything like that. Yet I hear it as a Jackie record, perfect 1960s diva pop that's up there with Dusty Springfield or Ann-Margret. It's a bootleg authored by her against her will, stolen from her like her husband, beyond her control, in the grand girl-group tradition of starlets who get trapped and manipulated by the Svengali producer, sort of like Ronnie and Phil Spector.

I put my Jackie record up on the kitchen stove so I could look at it all day. I left it in its protective plastic sleeve so food wouldn't get splattered on it. Since I never cooked anything but pasta on the stove, with tomato sauce out of jars, there were little red splotches all over the plastic sleeve. I liked the red splotches, yet felt guilty about not washing them away. When I had friends coming over I'd slip off the sleeve, and then Jackie was pure and pristine, on her white couch with the white curtains. When my friends left, I'd slip the cover back on, and she'd be spattered with blood all over again, corrupted by death, corrupted by being alive when her husband is dead, corrupted by knowing more than she's supposed to know about death.

I also have my grandmother's old copy of a quickie tribute mag, *Jacqueline Kennedy: Woman of Valor*. It reports, "Mrs. Kennedy's appetite, never robust, has returned." There was a lot of widow gossip in that mag that made me wonder, especially concerning the whereabouts of her ring. She put it on her dead husband's hand in the hospital? Then how did she get it back? Did she get photographed without her ring on? What did his family think about that? After she put it back on, when did she stop wearing it? I studied this and the other magazines in my Jackie shrine:

Screen Stories, April 1965: "Jackie Pleads, If You Love Me, Please Leave Me Alone!" The article notes, "Many people have wondered why she was not at his grave at Christmastime."

TV and Screenworld, March 1970: "Exclusive: Liz and Jackie's Spending War!" The story has this scoop: "The two richest and most glamorous women in the world are having the most expensive cat fight ever known in history." Liz bought the $1.05 million Krupp diamond, which Jackie wanted for her fortieth birthday; Jackie had to settle for $40,000 "Apollo 11" gold earrings from Aristotle Onassis, in the shape of the moon and the spaceship. According to the story, "Jackie, ever ready with the *bon mot*, chortled to actress Katina Paxinou, 'Ari was actually apologetic about them. But he promised me that if I'm good next year he'll give me the moon itself!' "

I immersed myself in Jackie trash like I was studying with a kung fu master. Did I learn anything? No way. But all the things you *want* to learn from grief turn out to be the total opposite of what you actually learn. There are no revelations, no wisdoms as a trade-off for the things you have lost. You just get stupider, more selfish. Colder and grimmer. You forget your keys. You leave the house and panic that you won't remember where you live. You know less than you ever did. You keep crossing thresholds of grief and you think, Maybe this one will unveil some sublime truth about life and death and pain. But on the other side, there's just more grief.

On the eleventh of every month, my friend Elizabeth would say, "Well, we made it through another month. So do we get her back now?" We always giggled, but we really did expect to get her back. It's not human to let go of love, even when it's dead. We expected one of these monthly anniversaries to be the Final Goodbye. We figured that we'd said all our goodbyes, and given up all the tears we had to give. We'd passed the test and would get back what we'd lost. But instead, every anniversary it hurt more, and every anniversary it felt like she was further away from coming back. The idea that there wouldn't be a final goodbye—that was a hard goodbye to say in itself and, at that point, still an impossible goodbye. No private eye has to tell you it's a long goodbye.

You tell yourself, I'll get to the end of this. But there's no finish line, just more doors to pass through, more goodbyes to say. You know that Smiths song "Girlfriend in a Coma"? At the end of the song, Morrissey whispers his last goodbye. I love that part; that line cracks me up now. Yeah, right, you *think* it's your last goodbye. He has no idea how many more he's got left. Good luck, kid.

Ralph Waldo Emerson knew the score: "I grieve that grief

can teach me nothing." That's from "Experience," his late essay about human loss and his son's death. There's a lot of cold-blooded shit in that essay, and the winter after Renée died I read it over and over. I always had to stop to butt my head against that sentence: "I grieve that grief can teach me nothing." I was hoping that was a lie. But it wasn't. Whatever I learn from this grief, none of it will take me any closer to what I want, which is Renée, who is gone forever. None of my tears will bring her closer to me. I can fit other things into the space she used to occupy, but whether I choose to do that, her absence from that space is permanent. No matter how good I get at being Renée's widower, I won't get promoted to being her husband again. The loss doesn't go away—it just gets bigger the longer you look at it.

It's the same with people who say, "Whatever doesn't kill you makes you stronger." Even people who say this must realize that the exact opposite is true. What doesn't kill you maims you, cripples you, leaves you weak, makes you whiny and full of yourself at the same time. The more pain, the more pompous you get. Whatever doesn't kill you makes you incredibly annoying.

That's part of why I worship Jackie. She just kept the story going. After she died, she went straight to the top of the charts, as the world's second-most-famous dead person. Jackie had no manager, but she went right on being the national widow, the way Elvis continued as the King after he died, with a legendary heart full of affection for America and all the grieving nobodies in it. She owns the name Jackie in a way her husband could never own his. When you say Jack, most people probably think of Nicholson, the closest thing to a default Jack in American pop culture, but Jackie Kennedy owns Jackie, despite the gentlemen named Robinson, Chan, Stewart, or Earle Haley. When Tammy Wynette died, The Nashville Network did a tribute special in which the singer Marty Stuart mused, "I bet she's hanging out right now with Jackie O." I thought this was a shockingly beautiful thing to say. Tammy and Jackie didn't exactly come from the same neighborhood. In life, Jackie wasn't what you'd call down home; Loretta Lynn sang about her as a celebrity snob in the 1970 hit "One's on the Way." I'm sure Tammy felt the same. But in death, Jackie can be anything we want her to be, even a country star. She has red blood on her pink dress, but she's wild and blue.

glossin' and flossin'

A SIDE ONE DATE/TIME	**B** SIDE TWO DATE/TIME
Indeep: "Last Night a DJ Saved My Life"	• Fleetwood Mac: "Gold Dust Woman"
Sugar Ray: "Ode to the Lonely Hearted"	• Ozzy Osbourne: "Flying High Again"
Aerosmith: "No More No More"	• Stevie Wonder: "Boogie on Reggae
Rolling Stones: "She's So Cold"	• Woman"
T. Rex: "Bang a Gong (Get It On)"	• Abba: "SOS"
Frankie Valli: "Can't Take My Eyes off	• Paul Mauriat: "Love Is Blue"
You"	• OutKast: "Rosa Parks"
English Beat: "Save It for Later"	• Jay-Z and Jermaine Dupri: "Money
Prince: "I Wanna Be Your Lover"	• Ain'ta Thing"
Dusty Springfield: "I Just Don't Know	• Rolling Stones: "Emotional Rescue"
What to Do with Myself"	• Mase featuring Total: "What You
Abba: "Mamma Mia"	• Want"
Heart: "Magic Man"	• Hüsker Dü: "Never Talking to You
Vanessa Williams: "The Comfort Zone"	• Again"
	• Rolling Stones: "Waiting on a Friend"

When you want to start living, what do you
do? How do you start? Where do you go? Who do you need
to blow?

I wanted to start. That was something. But what do you do
with a desire like that? I didn't know, so I did nothing with it. I

had been a widower for over a year and the second year was rougher than the first. I had done nothing with 1998, and had no ambitions for 1999 except getting it over with as fast as possible. Given another year that Renée didn't get, I planned to waste it. I made no plans to make things better. All I did was sit in my empty yard. Planet earth was blue, nothing left to do. Planet earth was pink, nothing left to drink.

I looked for spiritual solace in *Chained Heat 2*, arguably the finest straight-to-video women's-prison flick of the early nineties (nosing out *Caged Heat 2: Stripped of Freedom*). Brigitte Nielsen plays Magda Kasar, the sadistic warden. You see, after the fall of Communism, they have empty prisons in Eastern Europe, so the sadistic wardens need to rustle up fresh prisoners. This is where innocent American girls come in. Innocent American girls who foolishly fall asleep on trains, allowing Brigitte Nielsen's agents to plant drugs on them, setting up phony busts so Brigitte Nielsen can brush the hair out of their eyes with her riding crop (all sadistic wardens carry those, to handle insolent prisoners with hair in their eyes) and murmur, "Mmmm—your skin is so pink." This is all in the first five minutes. They played it a lot on the USA Network around three A.M., when everybody who had a reason to fall asleep, or a way of getting there, was gone for the night and it was just us inmates, watching in our cells.

I would watch *Chained Heat 2*, or some other movie, and lie on the couch hoping I would fall asleep. If I tried lying in bed, I would hyperventilate and my heart would start beating too fast, until I would have to breathe into a paper bag. The worse the movie was, the more it cheered me up. I was grateful to stumble across *Witchblade*, featuring Julie Strain as a creature of the dark who feeds on the blood of gangsters. Or was it *Witchboard 2: The Devil's Doorway*? I know—it was *Witchcraft IV: The Virgin Heart*. There's a scene where one of the gangsters asks, "What time is it?" The other one says, "What, do I look like Big Ben? Am I Swiss? Am I ticking?" I was grateful to resume hyperventilating, just to drown out the dialogue. If I was lucky, I got to sleep before dawn; if not, I knew there were at least three other *Witchcraft* movies out there somewhere.

On one such night, I decided I was having a pulmonary embolism. There was no other explanation for the way I felt. I waited until six, when I thought the emergency room would open for business. I drank some bourbon, figuring that would either slow down the heart attack or make me too clumsy to die right. I raided the boxes in the bathroom closet, looking for some kind of medication that might come in handy, and found some Stelazine from 1986. I watched MTV all night and held on to my paper bag. Eventually I said Fuck it and started walking to the hospital, since it was too cold for the car to start. If they weren't open, I'd just get in line and wait. I walked along the train tracks, paper bag in hand, clutching a throw pillow to my chest with the other arm, with the dawn over my head, and sat in the emergency room. Dr. Lutz was incredibly kind to me. She was so kind, I wanted to cry with humiliation that I was taking up her time when all I would do was let her down, the way I let down every other person trying to be kind to me. All she was going to get out of this was a reminder that some people aren't worth the trouble of being kind to, because they have neither the brains nor the power to make something for themselves out of your kindness. But I was standing right there, with electric wires hooked up to my chest, and it was too late to protect her from me.

My EKG proved I wasn't having a pulmonary embolism. It was so good, in fact, that the doctors were handing it around and complimenting it as if I had just done my first finger-painting. Dr. Lutz asked, "Has there been any major stress in your life lately?" I went, "Ummm . . ." She sent me home with a handful of Xanax, a bottle of Mylanta, and my word that I would do a little better to make some changes. That was a start. I walked down to the train tracks and headed home. That was a start, too.

Christmas was coming. Everybody in my family was dreading it, so we decided to flee to Florida. We could swim in the pool and drink margaritas at the Astro-Lanes Bowling Lounge in Nokomis and cheer one another up until it was safe to return to the world. This was a really excellent plan. (Christmas is like the "Hey Jude" of holidays—every five years, at one-third the length, it would be a perfectly nice idea.)

As I flew down to Tampa, I watched the old couple in the next row doing a crossword together. I watched them the whole way, even though I hate crosswords, because I hate planes more. He was a lot slower than she was. Her vision was better, so she read the clues out loud and tapped his serving tray impatiently while he made his guesses. He spoke very slowly and loudly. The idea that Renée and I were never going to be these people made me furious, until I could feel my heart pound with rage against my chest. I felt better once I got to the Tampa airport. The walls were a bright 1970s orange, like a Houston Astros uniform from the days when J. R. Richards was their pitcher, and everything looked shiny and cheery. I felt even better when I caught up with my sisters and parents in the airport. I realized I was starved for some color and noise, and I knew that's what I would get.

My sister Tracey was pregnant with the first grandchild in the family. It was very exciting. We assumed she was doing this to provide us with entertainment. Just for fun, Ann explained to her what an episiotomy is. As a biology teacher, Ann is a pro at explaining these things—pro enough to drain all the color from Tracey's face. Tracey was standing there in the pool, shaking her head, while Ann and Caroline swam around her, nodding. Tracey turned to me and said, "Rob? It's not true, is it?" But I was staying the hell out of that one. Tracey was reading a book called *What to Expect When You're Expecting*. I told her they should do a special edition for her called *What to Demand When You're Demanding*. The girls took turns playing rounds of "how to exhaust when you're exhausting" and "who to madden when you're maddening." It was a good time. It didn't make us all better or anything, but it was a start.

Tracey surprised her husband, Bryant, with a mix CD as a Christmas gift. This was the first mix CD any of us had seen, and we crowded around to gape at it. There was definitely a sense that the mix tape as we knew it was going through a major change. She titled it *Mackey Music*, filled it with his favorite Shawn Mullins and Garth Brooks songs, and put a picture of him on the cover. We were all wicked impressed at this technological breakthrough and got to know the mix extremely well when it went into heavy poolside rotation. But a clear advantage of mix tapes made itself immediately clear: Each side of the tape goes on for forty-five minutes, and then comes to a stop, allowing a chance for somebody to discreetly change the music, whereas a mix CD has only one side. Which means it goes on for eighty minutes, and you can't turn it off halfway through without offering some sort of lame excuse, such as "Garth is singing about cocaine in this song and it's bad for the baby," or "Dave Matthews is mixing violin solos with saxophone solos and it's bad for the baby."

The house was cold when I got back home from Florida. I realized the house was always cold, and would stay cold no matter how long I stayed back. Am I Swiss? Am I ticking? Sometimes.

To get out of my cold house, I went to a New Year's party at Darius's house, the same night I made this tape. Usually, I made any excuse not to leave the house, so going to a party was a big deal for me. I caught a ride with the Glimmer Girl, a bassist friend of mine. Glimmer didn't come to town until after Renée died, and I wished they could have met—they would have wagged their tails over each other—but they never got the chance. Glimmer was brilliant at getting me out of the house. She always made me feel safe, something I was not used to feeling around other people. I guess she and her boyfriend used to fight a lot, so she'd always call my radio show to request sad songs like PJ Harvey's "Dry." She would talk me into going to see bands at Tokyo Rose, and once I forced myself out of the house, it was usually fun to go hang with her gaggle of glam glimmerettes. If I couldn't take it, I would just sneak away, and Glimmer Girl would never ask why.

This night was fun. We danced to old disco records. I was extremely happy to hear "Last Night a DJ Saved My Life." She'd never heard the song before, and she was astounded at how bouncy it made me. We sat on the front stairs and smoked. At one point, I leaned in to light her cigarette, but she was just putting on lipgloss.

She and her boyfriend gave me a ride home. I didn't feel like going to bed by myself and lying there freezing, so I put on a pot of coffee and started making this tape. I decided to make the tape, then sit in the backyard and listen to it on my Walkman while drinking more cigarettes and smoking another bourbon. It was only two A.M., and I banged it out by four, so I'd have time to listen to it twice by the time the sun rose at seven. The chair in the backyard was covered with ice, but I sat on it anyway.

This is a classic example of a tape that tries to ruin a bunch of great songs by reminding you of a time you would rather forget. Sometimes great tunes happen to bad times, and when the bad time is over, not all the tunes get to move on with you. (I made another tape that winter that began with Roxy Music's "Mother of Pearl," one of my favorite songs since I was sixteen, but I haven't been able to listen to it since. That tape was so agonizing to hear, it took all the other songs down with it. Louis Prima's "Banana Split for My Baby"? Come on! Great tune! But ruined.)

Individually, all the songs on this tape make me smile, but lined up in this order, they make me shudder. Listening to this tape is like going back somewhere I never belonged in the first place, and it's spooky to tiptoe back in. All these sad songs: "SOS," "I Just Don't Know What to Do With Myself," "No More No More," "She's So Cold." Stevie Nicks in "Gold Dust Woman," chanting "widow" over and over. Mick Jagger in "Emotional Rescue," sneering at a poor girl trapped in a rich man's house. Even the fun songs sound miserable here. In any other context, Heart's "Magic Man" fires my blood corpuscles with images of erotic abundance. Ann Wilson? Love her! Nancy Wilson? Like her lots! The album cover where they're wearing capes and feeding a goat on the pastures of their own mystical Salisbury Plain dream world? I'm so there. But on this tape, "Magic Man" sounds scary. The "Magic Man" is magic just because he's *unreal*. Surely he's in love with somebody dead, so he's too magic to fit into the real world. He's isolated from everybody around him, and his isolation is contagious, making him a vampire who turns everybody he touches into a cold shell of abandoned humanity. Yes, even the lustrously busty ladies of Heart!

(It's only now I realize that the lyrics of this song are all about drugs. How embarrassing that I never noticed it before.)

Don't go home with that magic man! I wanted to shake my Walkman, warn the Heart girls to run away. Don't trust him! He might be magic, but he's not very nice! He says he just wants to get high awhile, but he'll get you so high you can't come back down. He'll make you stay inside so long, it hurts your eyes to go out, so you'll spend whole years wasting away in his mansion. You'll lose your sense of time. You'll lose your appetite. When your mama cries on the phone, you won't understand a word she's saying. You'll just tell her, "Try to understand." And Mrs. Wilson isn't falling for that shit. Ann! Nance! Get the hell out of there! One smile from that magic man, and you're done. You'll be so fucking magic, you won't be real any more. He'll even set your lipgloss on fire.

I hoped Glimmer Girl and her boy were sleeping somewhere, young and safe and together. I hoped they were breathing hard into each other's hair. I hoped her feet were bumping into his shins. I hoped they were asleep and not thinking about any of the things I was thinking about, and I hoped they never would. I listened to this tape twice all the way through, and then hurried into the cold house before the sun started to rise. If I waited for the house to warm up before I tried to start something, I would never start anything.

blue ridge gold

APRIL 2000

A SIDE ONE DATE/TIME	**B** SIDE TWO DATE/TIME
Perez Prado: "Why Wait"	• Glen Campbell: "Wichita Lineman"
Elvis Presley: "Moonlight Swim"	• Nico: "These Days"
Ray Charles: "Wichita Lineman"	• Merle Haggard: "I Take a Lot of Pride
Nan Vernon: "Moon River"	• in What I Am"
The Standells: "Riot on Sunset Strip"	• Santo & Johnny: "Sleepwalk"
Nancy Sinatra: "These Boots Are Made	• Dressy Bessy: "Jenny Come On"
for Walkin'"	• Sweet: "Wig-Wam Bam"
April Stevens: "Teach Me Tiger"	• Shirley Ellis: "The Clapping Song"
Kyu Sakamoto: "Sukiyaki"	• Louis Prima and Keely Smith: "That
The Shadows: "Spring Is Nearly Here"	• Was a Big Fat Lie"
Neil Diamond: "I Am . . . I Said"	• Ella Mae Morse: "The House of Blue
Dean Martin: "Everybody Loves	• Lights"
Somebody Sometime"	• The Rooftop Singers: "Walk
The Dave Clark Five: "Catch Us If You	• Right In"
Can"	• Gloria Wood: "Hey Bellboy"
The Shangri-Las: "Bulldog"	• Petula Clark: "A Sign of the Times"
Louis Prima: "My Conchetta"	• Nellie Lutcher: "Fine Brown Frame"
Glen Campbell: "Gentle on My Mind"	• The Quin-Tones: "Down the Aisle of
The Tornados: "Telstar"	• Love"
Stereo Total: "Supergirl"	• Rosie and the Originals: "Angel
John Denver: "Thank God I'm a	• Baby"
Country Boy"	•
The Three Suns: "Delicado"	•

One *night I had a bit* of a revelation. I was up late, as usual, unable to sleep, drinking ginger ale and flipping channels, looking for something to soothe my nerves, the way a Discovery Channel panda forages for bamboo. This time I found something—a newsmagazine piece about a breaking news story in Milwaukee. I watched with awe and reverence. The story concerned a nacho dwarf. He was the most famous and successful nacho dwarf in Milwaukee—maybe the world. His job was walking around in a Mexican restaurant wearing an oversized sombrero with a brim full of tasty nachos. The crown of the sombrero held a cup of salsa. The nacho dwarf greeted the customers, shook hands, worked the room. He would invite everybody to sample the treats he had on his head. He was there to serve. He was there to honor the nacho-dwarf code.

Understandably, quite a few of his fellow dwarves felt this was a degrading and insulting gig. Steve Vento (for that was his name), a former car salesman (for that was his trade), disagreed. He proclaimed himself proud to be a nacho dwarf. But other dwarves complained angrily that he was perpetuating inhumane stereotypes and encouraging mistreatment of non-nacho dwarves. In fact, they were protesting the restaurant, demanding a boycott until the nacho dwarf was canned.

I watched this with intense fascination. They showed a clip from the Anthony Michael Hall movie *Johnny Be Good*, which apparently had a party scene that had inspired the whole nacho-dwarf thing. They showed the dwarf lawyer who was representing the protesters. And they showed the nacho dwarf himself, defending his profession. He implied that maybe the other dwarves were just a little jealous that they did not have the talent to make it as a nacho dwarf. They resented his success, so they were trying to drive a fellow dwarf out of work and into the gutter. Why, they were taking food right out of his mouth!

"We are not trying to take food out of Mr. Vento's mouth," said the lawyer. "We are merely trying to take it off his head."

And then, dear friends, at those words, a little light flickered in my mind. Some sort of divine revelation started to make itself clear before my eyes, and a voice began to articulate unto me the horrible truth: I needed to get out of the apartment more. No, I *really* needed to get out of the apartment more.

Maybe it was time to think about leaving Charlottesville. I loved it here, but there were serious changes I needed to make, and this was not the place to make them. It was too hard to keep living surrounded by so much of the past. I needed to go. I wanted to walk before they made me run. There was too much happening there that I couldn't share with Renée, and if I was going to keep living, I needed to move on to a new location. Charlottesville was always going to be her place. I wanted it to stay that way.

I had new friends in Charlottesville who didn't know Renée, although they'd all heard stories about her before I got the chance to bring her up for the first time. It was bittersweet making friends who never got to hang with her, especially when they were so cool they reminded me of her. It was kind of like that Sade song "Maureen," where she's sad her dead friend can't meet her new friends. I knew I needed to learn some manners about when it was okay to tell people stories about Renée, and when it was just too traumatic for them to hear about her. I didn't want to scare them away. I was trying to learn some of Renée's social finesse, to remember the way she used to put people at ease and make them feel free. That was just never my department, but I tried to get better at it.

I had a support system in Charlottesville that I felt crazy walking away from, and I was glad I had stayed as long as I had, but it was time to go. Most of my friends were now in New York, so I figured I'd go there, although friends in other towns lobbied—Stephanie called from San Francisco and read the sublet listings into my machine until the tape ran out. I set up a goodbye shelf, where I put things I needed to get rid of. If something sat on the goodbye shelf for a few days and I still got a pang when I looked at it sitting there, it wasn't ready to go yet.

I said goodbye to our dog Duane (who I gave away) and our favorite band Pavement (who broke up but whose members made excellent solo albums). Duane spent her last year with me barking and howling, wishing she were anywhere else; Pavement spent their last tour fighting onstage. At their final shows, the band members reportedly wore handcuffs onstage as symbols of their frustration. Each goodbye came with different levels of relief, guilt, and confusion, so I put them off as long as I could. But dogs need to run free, and so do guitarists. It wasn't right to hold them back. I had a lot of goodbyes left to say, to places and people and trees and radio stations.

For all of us who loved Renée, there were many goodbyes. At my friend Amanda's wedding that spring, two of Renée's best friends had a little meltdown in the ladies' room when they saw that they were both wearing bike shorts under their fancy dresses to keep their thighs from rubbing together, a trick they'd both learned from Renée. They stayed in the ladies' room and cried, while their husbands wondered what was going on. There were lots of moments like that for all of us—encounters with clothes, baseball, books, music. Every few years, I buy an old Stylistics record and think, Man, these guys were great, it's been way too long. I get it home, make it halfway through side one, and then file it away in the Whenever pile because Renée loved them and it is too hard. Maybe next year, maybe not. I also assumed I'd never be able to take listening to the Replacements again, but then I made a new friend in the summer of 1999 who wore a rubber band around her wrist with Paul Westerberg's name written on it. Her favorite song was "Unsatisfied" and she gave the song back to me, without knowing she was doing it, and soon I loved it as much as ever. You just never know.

When friends came down to visit from New York, they were amused by my deplorable car-radio tastes. I had become addicted to AM 1600, Cavalier Memories. The station was stuck in 1963, keeping me sane on the road with a steady sound track of Nancy Sinatra and Ray Charles and The Shangri-La's. They seemed to play "Moon River" every forty minutes. All weekend, we drove around in the mountains listening to Cavalier Memories, where we heard most of the songs on this tape. After they went home, I sent them a copy of the tape as a Blue Ridge souvenir. I decided this was my new favorite mix. I walked around with it all spring. I made sequels: *Blue Ridge Platinum*, *Blue Ridge Velvet*, *Blue Ridge Silver*, *Blue Ridge Turquoise*.

Cavalier Memories was the only station Renée and I could always get in the old LeBaron, which didn't have an FM dial, but now that I had a new car with a working radio, I just wanted to go back to my huckleberry friends on AM 1600. My appetite for this music was raging. Every time I was in the car, I heard all these great songs I'd never appreciated before. I'm sure I startled the other people at intersections whenever I would idle at a red light, screaming "I Am . . . I Said" using the rearview as a mike.

It was bittersweet getting to know these songs I never got to share with Renée. I mean, it was one thing to make new friends, and have to explain to them who Renée was, and how cool she was, and how much she loved Ricky Nelson and Shania Twain and Biggie Smalls, and so on. I figured that would always happen, since there are so many billions of new people. But it was a lonesome surprise to make new friends with songs. One day I turned on the ignition in the parking lot and heard Glen Campbell's "Gentle on My Mind," a song I'd known all my life and never paid any attention to, and fell totally in love with it. I bet Renée loved this song. We never heard it together, so I have no way of knowing. Now I loved this song, and there was no way to tell her about it. I found myself desperately trying to start a conversation with this song, introducing myself. "You don't know me, 'Gentle on My Mind,' but I'm sure you've met my wife. Let me tell you a thing or two about her. . . ."

I'd drive around town, running errands or just escaping the house, and sing harmony duets with a partner who wasn't there. I would picture Renée in the empty passenger seat, singing along with me. What the hell good is it to sing a Glen Campbell song to yourself? Nancy Sinatra, Perez Prado, Ella Mae Morse, Dean Martin—my mirror was getting jammed up with all my friends. I was desperate for them all to meet Renée. It was strange to fall back in love with really old songs, or to hear them for the first time and not get to hear Renée sing along with them.

I loved these songs, learned the tunes and the words, took them into my heart to stay. I had no idea what to *do* with them. But they were doing something with me. I had a lot of goodbyes to say. This was going to take time. I had time.

via vespucci

DECEMBER 2002

A SIDE ONE DATE/TIME	B SIDE TWO DATE/TIME
Elton John: "Mellow"	• Stevie Wonder: "Golden Lady"
John Lennon: "Oh My Love"	• Tom T. Hall: "I Miss a Lot of Trains"
Fairport Convention: "Tale in Hard Time"	• Lonnie Donegan: "Does Your Chewing Gum Lose Its Flavor (On the Bedpost Overnight)"
Gary Stewart: "Out of Hand"	•
Lou Christie: "Two Faces Have I"	• The Monkees: "Daydream Believer"
The Dovells: "Bristol Stomp"	• The Chordettes: "Mr. Sandman"
Martha and the Vandellas: "No More Tearstained Make Up"	• Lou Christie: "The Gypsy Cried"
Gary U.S. Bonds: "Quarter to Three"	• Swingin' Medallions: "Double Shot (Of My Baby's Love)"
Ron Wood: "Mystifies Me"	• Jive Fives: "Hully Gully Calling Time"
Jerry Butler: "For Your Precious Love"	• Ray Barretto: "El Watusi"
Elton John: "Dirty Little Girl"	• Freddy Cannon: "Palisades Park"
Beach Boys: "Johnny Carson"	• Chubby Checker: "The Fly"
Jerry Lee Lewis: "Whole Lotta Shakin'"	• Joe Jones: "You Talk Too Much"
Everly Brothers: "All I Have to Do Is Dream"	• Dion and the Belmonts: "Love Came to Me"
Five Americans: "Western Union"	• Brenda Lee: "Sweet Nothin's"
	• Tommy James & the Shondells: "Mirage"
	• Merrilee Rush and the Turnabouts: "Angel of the Morning"
	• Ohio Express: "Yummy Yummy Yummy"
	• Fats Domino: "I'm Walkin'"

I *made this tape while* moving into my new apartment in Brooklyn. The living room has a china cabinet, but I loaded it up with tapes instead of dishes, unpacking one box of cassettes after another. I still haven't finished unpacking—by the time I do, it'll be time to move again.

One of the things I love about my neighborhood is the junk shop on Manhattan Avenue that has a basement full of used vinyl. The store doesn't have a name, or a sign out front, but once you venture down the stairs, you're in a shrine. I have never seen so many records crammed into one room, ceiling to floor. They're not in any order, so it's a place to spend a winter day scavenging for buried treasure. After my first visit there, I took my armful of records home and made this tape. There are crackles and scratches everywhere. Some of the songs are old favorites, some are new to me. I had never even heard of Tommy James and the Shondells' "Mirage"—how did I possibly live so much of my life without that song? Martha and the Vandellas' *Watchout!*—how did I manage without that one?

I live in a new city, where I have found friends who never met Renée and only know her through me. My ears runneth over with new favorite songs, new favorite bands, new favorite people to share them with. I met a girl, an astrophysicist who moved here from Charlottesville, and fell in love. We met while I was visiting friends down there; I first heard her voice on the car radio, where she was doing a Pixies tribute show on WTJU as DJ

Astrogrrrl. She made me a mix for my birthday, a real cassette, although I couldn't read the label because she wrote it in Japanese. So many great songs: The Normal's "Warm Leatherette," Siouxsie's "Happy House," The Pixies' "Cactus," The Cure's "A Night Like This." Well, clearly this was nothing but good.

Ally Astrogrrrl and I listen to the iPod I gave her for her birthday, which is pink to match the winter coat she wears over her fishnets. Last Christmas she used it to DJ the NASA holiday party, blasting the Stooges and David Bowie until one of the other scientists came over to turn the volume down. On Friday nights, we go eat sushi and play pinball, while she feeds quarters into the jukebox to play Bauhaus and Sisters of Mercy, bands I used to hate until I met her. Her specialty is galactic structure—and I can't even find my way around McGuinness Boulevard. She explains the movements of the galaxies to me; she digs through her shoebox of high school tapes and plays me Skinny Puppy, Revolting Cocks, My Life with the Thrill Kill Kult, and other bands I never gave a damn about. They took Love and Rockets' "Ball of Confusion" off the jukebox at The Library on Avenue A because she wouldn't stop playing it. Her karaoke anthem is Nirvana's "Lithium."

On weekend afternoons, Astrogrrrl and I can hear my upstairs neighbor sing along with her favorite Queen song, which is "Don't Stop Me Now." She likes that song *a lot*. She never plays it just once. I didn't notice before, but it has the exact same lyrics as Eric B. and Rakim's "Follow the Leader." I don't know my upstairs neighbor's name, or where she's from, but I know she loves to hit those Freddy Mercury high notes and blast off. She had a boyfriend for a while who used to listen to folk music, but now he doesn't seem to be around anymore. She still has "Don't Stop Me Now," though. The cars outside of my window blast Polish hip-hop, 24/7. I'm literally surrounded by music.

Sometimes I run into old friends I haven't seen in years, who ask how Renée is—that still happens. Now it happens maybe once a year or so. They usually tell me a Renée story I haven't yet heard. I am always happy to hear her name. I was once at a house party in Brooklyn, waiting in line for the bathroom with a friend I didn't meet until a couple of years ago, when he randomly asked, "Hey, what was Renée's favorite Hank Williams song?" That made my night. (It was "Setting the Woods on Fire.") I meet new songs, too, and the new songs will sometimes bring her up. Renée told me about Gary Stewart's "Out of Hand" once, said it could have been written about us. I recently heard it for the first time. She was right.

I make new friends and hear their stories. Last fall, I was sitting at the kitchen table of two friends who have been together since 1972. They tell me a story about how they got together. She couldn't decide between two suitors, so she left New York City to spend the summer in an ashram. (Did I mention it was 1972?) One of the suitors sent her postcards while she was gone, the famous postcards that came inside the sleeve of the Rolling Stones' *Exile on Main Street*. Needless to say, he was the suitor who won her hand. They tell me this story, laughing and interrupting each other, as their teenage daughter walks through the kitchen on her way out to a Halloween party. I've heard of these postcards—over the years, I've heard plenty of record-collector guys boast that they own the original vinyl *Exile on Main Street* with the original postcards, intact and pristine in the virgin sleeve. I've never heard of *anybody* getting rid of their prized *Exile* postcards, much less actually writing on them and sending them through the mail to a girl. I watch these two, laughing over this story at the same kitchen table they've shared for thirty years. I realize that I will never fully understand the millions of bizarre ways that music brings people together.

I even met another young widower once, the only one I've met in eight years. We were in a sleazy West Village indie-rock bar, at the after-party for a Strokes show. He was the fiancé of a photographer I knew. We chatted about New York, and he asked why I'd moved here. I blurted out something about Virginia, where I used to live, when I was a husband, and then my wife died and I had to start over. He said, Uh, me, too.

We spent the whole night in a corner of the bar, breaking it all down. How did she die? When did you start sleeping again? When did you start eating again? Did people talk about it, or were they too scared? Do people avoid mentioning her around you? If they say "ex-wife," do you correct them? When does it stop hurting? Did her parents stay in touch? For how long afterward did you try living in the same house? Did you ever have that dream where you run into her on the street, and don't recognize her, and then you wake up and don't go back to bed for a week?

Neither of us had ever met another one of the species. We couldn't stop interrogating each other. All around us, people were dancing and guzzling Rolling Rocks and snorting bumps off their knuckles. His fiancée kept dancing over to check on us. We knew we were being rude, but we also knew we'd never get another chance to have this conversation.

After Renée died, I assumed the rest of my life would be just a consolation prize. I would keep living, and keep having new experiences, but none of them would compare to the old days. I would have to settle for a lonely life I didn't want, which would always remind me of the life I couldn't have anymore. But it didn't turn out that way, and there's something strange and upsetting about that. I would have stayed in 1996 if I could have, but it wasn't my choice, so now I have to move either forward or back—it's up to me. Not changing isn't an option. And even though I've changed in so many ways—I'm a different person with a different life—the past is still with me every minute.

Last summer I took all of Renée's hats to Central Park. I walked around the Great Lawn, leaving a hat every few benches. I thought of leaving a note on each hat saying, "This belonged to somebody very cool who loved hats, although she hardly ever wore them after the day she bought them, don't get me started, and she loved this park, although she only came here once, in 1992, and we heard some guy with a banjo playing 'Take Me Home Country Roads' and she laughed because this guy had no idea he was getting a chance to sing it for a real West Virginian girl." But none of the hats were big enough for a story that long.

So I just put a yellow sticky note on each one, saying, "Free." There was the dark green bowler with the black velvet trim, the soft green cotton sun-hat she wore when we were walking around Dingle Bay in Ireland, the crimson cloche made of hemp fiber. There was the pink pillbox that she bought in a Salvation Army in North Carolina, with the mildew on it that made her sneeze. There were two different straw hats, one of which she wore to a barbeque lunch our wedding weekend, except I could no longer remember which one. I walked from bench to bench, trying not to be noticed as I left each hat, vaguely expecting to get stopped by cops and taken downtown for suspicious headgear disposal. The harder I tried not to look criminal, the harder my heart pounded and the faster I walked. After dropping off the last hat, I did a few loops around the statue of King Jagiello, who led Poland and Lithuania to victory over the Teutonic Knights at the Battle of Grunwald in 1410. I worried that some of the hats were not beautiful enough for anybody to want to wear them. They would get left behind; they would be forgotten. But I headed back to the Great Lawn twenty minutes later, and of course there were no hats left on the benches. The hats were free.

There's a lot I miss about the nineties. It was an open, free time of possibilities, changes we thought were permanent. It seemed inconceivable that things would ever go back to the way they were in the eighties, when monsters were running the country and women were only allowed to play bass in indie-rock bands. The nineties moment has been stomped over so completely, it's hard to imagine it ever happened, much less that it lasted five, six, seven years. Remember Brittany Murphy, the funny, frizzy-haired, Mentos-loving dork in *Clueless*? By 2002, she was the hood ornament in *8 Mile*, just another skinny starlet, an index of everything we've lost in that time.

When Avril Lavigne sings "Sk8tr Boi," a song about how lucky she is to wait backstage for her rock boy, how is anybody supposed to remember that the Avril Lavignes of yesteryear were sold pop fantasies in which *they* had a place onstage, too? ("Sk8tr Boi" is a great song, too—which is part of the reason why there's nothing simple about these questions.) Something was happening in nineties music that isn't happening *anywhere* in pop culture these days, with women making noise in public ways that seem distant now. Nirvana brought mass appeal back to guitar rock, and the mass appeal made the bands braver— some of them even had something to say about the real world, which is way more than anybody has a right to expect from musicians. A kind of popular song existed that didn't before and doesn't any more, as arty guitar bands seized the moment to communicate with huge numbers of fans and go to extremes and indulge their appalling drug-addled muses and say dangerous or dumb things and expand the emotional/musical languages with which people communicated.

I remember the summer of 1996, at a drunken wedding with one of my professors, a Hendrix-freak baby boomer, when he was complaining about the "bullet-in-the-head rock and roll" the kids were listening to today, and he asked Renée, "What does rock and roll have today that it didn't have in the sixties?"

Renée said, "Tits," which in retrospect strikes me as not a bad one-word off-the-dome answer at all. The nineties fad for indie rock overlapped precisely with the nineties fad for feminism. The idea of a pop culture that was pro-girl, or even just not anti-girl—that was a 1990s mainstream dream, rather than a 1980s or 2000s one, and it was real for a while. Music was not just part of it but leading the way—hard to believe, hard even to remember. But some of us do.

America is a different place than it was in the nineties, when peace and prosperity and freedom were here to stay. The radio has become homogenized, with practically every station around the country bought up and programmed by the same corporation, and in a shocking coincidence, the weird girls have been shoved back underground. The economy is in the toilet. The war is here to stay. Since the coup of 2000, those nineties dreams have been stomped down so hard it seems crazy to remember that they were real, or at least part of real lives. I keep my friends around, try to stay close to them, try to treat them right. I try to stay in touch with my friends who are far away, and I do a bad job of that, but I carry them with me.

I recently met a girl, a friend of a friend, and it took me only a minute to recognize her—she was Melissa, from the John Fluevog shoe store in Boston, where Renée would go to look for cool shoes. She'd helped Renée find three of her all-time top five pairs of shoes. I'd never even learned her name, but I remembered her kindness, and I remembered the way she talked about her cool indie-rock drummer boyfriend, who is now her husband and touring with the Dixie Chicks. At first, I felt strange telling her why I remembered her, or that my wife had been buried in shoes she'd helped pick out, but she got it. I told her about the day Renée bought the platform mod creepers and walked down Newbury Street, saying, "Nobody in Charlottesville has shoes this cool. None of the skinny girls have shoes this cool. That skinny Lori from Georgia doesn't have shoes this cool."

If I didn't want to have these experiences, didn't want to run into living things that reminded me of the past, I would have to hide under a rock—except that would remind me of the past, too, so I try not to hide. What shocks me is that the present is alive. It wouldn't have shocked Renée.

I depend on my friends to remind me that what started in the nineties isn't all dead, and the struggles of those years are not all lost, and the future is unwritten. Astrogrrrl and I go see our favorite local bar band, the Hold Steady, every time they play. They always end with our favorite song, "Killer Parties," and sometimes I think, man, all the people I get to hear this song with, we're going to miss each other when we die. When we die, we will turn into songs, and we will hear each other and remember each other.

A lot of my music friends don't touch cassettes anymore; they stick to MP3s. I love my iPod, too—completely love it. I love my iPod carnally. I would rather have sex with my iPod than with

Jennifer Lopez. (I wouldn't have to hear the iPod whine about getting its hair rumpled.) But for me, if we're talking about romance, cassettes wipe the floor with MP3s. This has nothing to do with superstition, or nostalgia. MP3s buzz straight to your brain. That's part of what I love about them. But the rhythm of the mix tape is the rhythm of romance, the analog hum of a physical connection between two sloppy, human bodies. The cassette is full of tape hiss and room tone; it's full of wasted space, unnecessary noise. Compared to the go-go-go rhythm of an MP3, mix tapes are hopelessly inefficient. You go back to a cassette the way a detective sits and pours drinks for the elderly motel clerk who tells stories about the old days—you know you might be somewhat bored, but there might be a clue in there somewhere. And if there isn't, what the hell? It's not a bad time. You know you will waste time. You plan on it.

All mixes have their mutations, whether it's the *mmmmm* of the cassette or the *krrriiissshhh* of the MP3. There is no natural religion, as William Blake would say. No matter how hard you listen, you can't get down to the pure sound, not as it gets heard by impure flesh-and-blood ears. So instead of listening to the pure sound, you listen to a mix. When you try to play a song in your memory, and you remember how it goes, you're just making an imperfect mix of it in your mind. Human sound is mutant sound. You listen, and you mutate along with the sound.

Not long ago I was walking through my neighborhood and found a box of tapes on the sidewalk, set out for the trash. Of course I took them home. They were Polish disco mix tapes for the most part, as well as Ricky Martin and Shania Twain and Jennifer Paige cassingles. There was also an Ace of Base cassingle I'd never heard before—from 1998. What the hell were they doing still making Ace of Base cassingles in 1998? But my favorite of these tapes is called *Mega Disco*. It includes "Let It Whip," "Groove Line," "Shame, Shame, Shame," and "You Sexy Thing." I've heard this last song on so many mixes over the years. It's a different song every time, but the same thing always happens. You hear something you like, and you press rewind to go back to it. But you can't rewind the tape to the exact same place again. So you start fresh.

What is love? Great minds have been grappling with this question through the ages, and in the modern era, they have come up with many different answers. According to the Western philosopher Pat Benatar, love is a battlefield. Her paisan Frank Sinatra would add the corollary that love is a tender trap. The stoner kids who spent the summer of 1978 looking cool on the hoods of their Trans Ams in the Pierce Elementary School parking lot used to scare us little kids by blasting the Sweet hit "Love Is Like Oxygen"—you get too much, you get too high, not enough and you're gonna die. Love hurts. Love stinks. Love bites, love bleeds, love is the drug. The troubadours of our times all agree: They want to know what love is, and they want you to show them.

But the answer is simple. Love is a mix tape.

acknowledgments

No man does it all by himself, as the Village People once sang, and they should know. So! Thank you to everybody who helped with this book. My editor Carrie Thornton is a goddess and a true Virginia girl; I am grateful for her brilliance. My agent Daniel Greenberg rocks like Side Three of *Exile in Main Street*, contributing an infinite supply of insight and energy from the start. He also picked out a stray sentence from one of my early drafts, and said, "There's your title." Joe Levy has been exchanging mix tapes and arguments with me since the days of Tiffany and Big Daddy Kane, and nobody could be a more heroic presence in my life—he lived through this book with me twice, and neither time would have been possible without him. Thank you, Joe.

All love and worship to Ally Polak. None of this could have been written without her constant love and support and feline soul. Stay on my arm, you little charmer.

Thanks to my family: all Sheffields, Mackeys, Hanlons, Twomeys, Courtneys, Moriartys, O'Briens, Durfers, Govers,

Crists, Hugharts, Smiths, Vieras, and Needhams. I owe everything to my mom and dad, Bob and Mary Sheffield. Thank you for your wisdom, for inspiration, and for still necking in the kitchen to the Del-Vikings. Thank you to my glorious sisters Ann, Tracey, and Caroline; Bryant, Charlie, Sarah, Allison, David, John, Sydney, and Jack; Donna, Joe, Sean, Jake, Tony, and Shirley; Jonathan, Kari-Ann, Ashley, Amber; Drema, Ruby, and Joe Gross. All my love and thanks to Buddy and Nadine Crist, for endless support and kindness.

Thank you everybody at Crown, especially Steve Ross, Brandi Bowles, Kristin Kiser, Meghan Wilson, Lauren Dong, Laura Duffy, Dan Rembert, Donna Passannante, and Jill Flaxman.

Big up to all at *Rolling Stone* past and present, especially the great Will Dana, James Kaminsky, Nathan Brackett, Elizabeth Goodman, Lauren Gitlin, Bob Love, David Swanson, Austin Scaggs, Jason Fine, David Fricke, Mark Binelli, Jancee Dunn. Tom Nawrocki has permanently changed my outlook on America (not the country) and Bread (not the food). I idolize Jenny Eliscu, but doesn't everybody? Hell, I idolize myself just for knowing her.

Very special thanks and respect to Jann Wenner, man of wealth and taste, for always letting it bleed.

Gavin Edwards, you know you are the man—your help on this book doesn't even make the Top Forty reasons why you rock (liking Belinda Carlisle's "I Get Weak," however, comes in at Number Thirty-Eight); Darcey Steinke, who was Renée's hero, and is now mine, from whom I never stop learning; Chuck

Klosterman (god of thunder); Robert Christgau and Carola Dibbell (if music writers were farmers, Christgau would be the guy who invented the plow); Marc Spitz; Niki Kanodia; Jeffrey Stock; Marc Weidenbaum; Stephanie "MMMBop" Wells; Greil Marcus (as Renée said, "he's the only Yankee I've ever met who knows how to pronounce 'Appalachian'"); all Virginia friends around the world: Elizabeth Outka, Lia Rushton, La Contessa Susan Lentati, Erin Rodriguez, Merit Wolfe, Stephanie Bird, Jeanine Cassar O'Rourke, their families; Charles W. Taylor III and everybody at WTJU, the greatest radio station on the planet, as you can hear yourself at wtju.net; Tyler Magill (for redefining the Britpop haircut), Carey Price (the chicktator), Sarah Wyatt (she bangs the drums), Motel No-Tell UK, The Curious Digit, Plan 9 Records; Sarah Wilson; Jill Beifuss; Karl Precoda.

The musical ideas in this book got shaped in the insane fanzine world of the eighties and nineties, when zines had staples in the spine and no bandwidth at all. Thank you to my fanzine gurus, especially Phil "Frankie Five Angels" Dellio (*Radio On*), Frank Kogan (*Why Music Sucks*), Chuck Eddy (everywhere).

A passionate round of applause for: Nils Bernstein, Jennie Boddy, Caryn Ganz, Radha Metro, Melissa Eltringham, Heather Rosett, Katherine Profeta, Jen Sudul, Strummer Edwards, Asif Ahmed, Tracey Pepper, Pam Renner, Chris McDonnell, Ted Friedman, Flynn Monks, Graine Courtney, Laura Larson, Craig Marks, Rene Steinke, Sarah Lewitinn, John Leland, Neva Chonin, James Hannaham, Laura Sinagra, Jon Dolan, Walter T.

Smith, Joshua Clover, Eric Weisbard, Ann Powers, Sasha Frere-Jones, Jon Bing, Paul Outka, Ivan Kreilkamp, Jen Fleissner, Erik Pedersen, Sister Pat, David Berman, Kembrew McLeod, Ed Pollard, The Nadine Crew, The Softies, The Secret Stars, The Hold Steady, and everyone else who has helped. Elizabeth Mitchell said the right thing at the right time. So did Mike Viola, and if you like this book, you will also probably like the Candy Butchers' album *Hang On Mike*. Thank you Joey Ramone for being nice to Renée for a few minutes in 1993. Thank you to all famous people, everywhere, especially the rock stars, plus the BVM and all the angels and saints. Thank you St. Jude. God bless Mother Nature, she's a single woman, too.

Always: David and Bridie Twomey; Ray and Peggy Sheffield.

Thanks to Dump for my favorite song, "International Airport," and to everybody who's ever listened to it on a mix tape from me. I don't think it's anybody else's favorite song yet, but you never know.

about the author

ROB SHEFFIELD is a
contributing editor at *Rolling Stone*,
where he writes the "Pop Life"
column. His work has appeared in
the *Village Voice*, *Spin*, *Slate*, *Details*,
Radio On, *The Literary Review*, and
many other publications. He has also
written for MTV and has appeared
on various VH1 and MTV shows.
He lives in Brooklyn.